THE NEW LASAGNA COOKBOOK

ALSO BY MARIA BRUSCINO SANCHEZ

Sweet Maria's Cookie Jar:
100 Favorite, Essential Recipes for Everyone Who Loves Cookies

Sweet Maria's Italian Desserts:
Classic and Casual Recipes for Cookies, Cakes, Pastry, and Other Favorites

Sweet Maria's Italian Cookie Tray: A Cookbook

Sweet Maria's Cake Kitchen:
Classic and Casual Recipes for Cookies, Cakes, Pastry, and Other Favorites

THE NEW

Lasagna

COOKBOOK

~~~

A Crowd-Pleasing Collection of Recipes from

Around the World for the Perfect One-Dish Meal

Maria Bruscino Sanchez

ST. MARTIN'S PRESS ❧ NEW YORK

Photos © Scott Goodwin
Food styling by Travis Grandon

www.stmartins.com

Design by Maggie Goodman

Library of Congress Cataloging-in-Publication Data
Sanchez, Maria Bruscino.
    The new lasagna cookbook : a crowd-pleasing collection of recipes from around the
world for the perfect one-dish meal / by Maria Bruscino Sanchez.—1st ed.
        p. cm.
    ISBN-13: 978-0-312-36782-4
    ISBN-10: 0-312-36782-1
    1. Cookery (Pasta) 2. Cookery, International. I. Title.
    TX809.M17S227 2008
    641.8'22—dc22

                                                                            2008020579

First Edition: September 2008

10 9 8 7 6 5 4 3 2 1

~~~

For Mom and Dad, who taught me

the importance of good food

and how to share it

CONTENTS

ACKNOWLEDGMENTS

Many thanks to my agent, Carla Glasser. She believed in this book from the beginning and encouraged me to write it.

My editor, Michael Flamini, for his enthusiasm and appetite for lasagna. Vicki Lame, and everyone at St. Martin's who helped shape and develop the book: Sally Richardson, George Witte, Jeffrey Capshew, Jane Liddle, Cheryl Mamaril, Maggie Goodman, and Tara Cibelli.

Thanks to Scott Goodwin and Travis Grandon for the amazing photos and styling.

The staff at Sweet Maria's for their hard work and sense of humor.

The biggest thanks to "The Monday Night Lasagna Club": Edgar, Tom, and Richard for their encouragement, sampling, and honest opinions.

INTRODUCTION

I've always been passionate about lasagna. Hot, saucy, and cheesy, it's been one of my favorite dishes. During a random discussion a few years ago with my agent, Carla, I mentioned my growing obsession with this delicious layered pasta. Being a baker by day, I began to notice definite similarities between making lasagna and making cakes. Both have three basic components that combine to create a singular sensation. All of a sudden I began to see sauce as frosting, fillings as fillings, and noodles as cake layers. At last my obsession was clear and this cookbook was born.

Technically "lasagna" refers to the long broad noodles that are fresh or dried, boiled, layered, and baked to create a "lasagne," which is the plural form of lasagna. (In this book we will use the common term "lasagna" to refer to the entire baked finished pasta.) In the fourteenth century, the first recipe for lasagna appeared in an anonymous Italian cookbook.

For all its complexity here in the U.S., lasagna in Italy is relatively simple. Ultrafresh ingredients combine with simplicity of flavors. Creamy béchamel, a hearty ragu, and a generous grating of pecorino or Parmesan are usually the main components. As with most Italian cooking, every region has its own special lasagna. The north is known for its rich white sauces, the south for its fresh tomatoes and mozzarella. The birthplace of lasagna, Bologna, is in the heart of Italy's famous food region Emilia-Romagna. Here you'll find the queen of all sauces, Bolognese. Other classic lasagnas from this region include a gut-busting one filled with tortellini and mortadella. Here in the U.S., some people dislike lasagna because all they have ever eaten has been over-sauced, overly cheesy, greasy versions from an Italian chain restaurant or their super-market freezer. It's time to make and enjoy a true lasagna.

My Italian-American experience is filled with family gatherings. Sundays and holidays are often the days to share meals and stories. Lasagna is a popular item for these meals because it's a great make-ahead party food. It's also one of the first dishes I learned to make once I got out on my own.

No one makes and eats lasagna alone (leftovers, sure); its primary purpose is to be shared. From the warm gooey center to the crusty corner pieces, everyone has a favorite lasagna spot. The right amounts of sauce, filling, and noodle combine to create the ultimate Italian comfort food.

Getting yourself organized by making either one or all of the lasagna components ahead of time can make assembling the lasagna a less daunting task. So many people dislike lasagna because of the amount of work that it takes to put it all together, but it's so worth the effort when the perfect mix of pasta, creamy filling, and tasty sauce come together for this classic dish. Most sauces can be frozen for weeks and thawed before using. Many of the fillings can be made one day in advance, and assembly of the lasagna can be done a day in advance of serving.

If you already love lasagna this book will challenge the way you think about lasagna.

Not all lasagnas are baked whole in a casserole dish. Think outside the Pyrex and try one of the "free-form" lasagnas such as the elegant Lobster with Roasted Red Pepper Sauce or the Lasagna Caprese, my interpretation of the classic salad that becomes an individual stack of ruffle-edged lasagna noodles, fresh tomato, mozzarella, and basil. Not all of these lasagnas feature Italian flavors. I offer a world of flavors from Middle Eastern lasagna with spices and phyllo to a flavor-packed Cajun chicken lasagna layered with Cheddar cheese and flour tortillas. Lasagna can be a *primi piatti*, or first course, as often served in Italy, or it can be a main dish. The combination of flavors is endless and delicious. This book is a collection of my favorite flavors. Hopefully, it will offer guidelines and inspire you to create your own lasagnas. Paired with a favorite wine, fresh salad, fruit, and a little something sweet, lasagna makes a perfect meal. Add a healthy serving of friends, family, and conversation and enjoy.

INGREDIENT TIPS

~~~~~~~

Here are a few of the essential ingredients used in making lasagnas.

Cheese

PARMESAN:
This thick, hard cow's milk cheese is aged at least two years. It has a mellow and nutty flavor. The finest is Parmigiano-Reggiano. Buy it in wheels or wedges and freshly grate it when needed.

PECORINO ROMANO:
A sharp, aged sheep's milk cheese. Look for wheels or wedges of pecorino Romano and freshly grate as needed.

RICOTTA:
This light, soft-curd cheese literally means "recooked." It's made from the whey produced when making other cheeses such as mozzarella or provolone.

RICOTTA SALATA:
Aged, hard, salted ricotta.

GORGONZOLA:
A flavorful creamy, blue-veined cheese.

FONTINA:
Creamy, mild, semisoft cow's milk cheese.

MOZZARELLA:
Mild Italian soft cheese traditionally made from water buffalo's milk is *mozzarella di bufala*. This can be very hard to find. Many excellent brands, now made from cow's milk, are more readily available and sold packed in water. This type is commonly called *fior di latte,* literally "flower of milk." It is fresh and perfect for most of the recipes in this book. Try to avoid packaged mozzarella.

Cooking Spray
Nonstick cooking spray is essential to be sure your lasagna doesn't stick to the bottom, sides, and corners of the baking dish.

Flour
For fresh pasta making, Italian double zero (00) flour will yield the most consistent results. The double zero refers to how finely the flour is ground. It is a soft white flour, with less gluten. All-purpose unbleached flour will work fine in the fresh pasta as well as in the béchamel sauce recipes. Semolina is used in commercial pasta production, not by the home chef.

Garlic

I use fresh garlic only, not peeled cloves soaked in olive oil. Look for large unsprouted bulbs, without green or dry spots.

Herbs

Fresh herbs, not dried, will give your lasagna fillings and sauces the fullest flavor.

Flat-leaf Italian-style parsley has the best flavor. Look for green, unblemished leaves of basil.

Olive Oil

Extra virgin olive oil comes from the first pressing of olives without heat or chemicals and provides a fresher, more pungent flavor. Pressings vary in color and strength. It's best to experiment and find the brands that your personal palate prefers. Italian brands vary from region to region. There are many great olive oils from other countries such as Spain and Lebanon.

Pancetta

This is flavorful Italian-style bacon cured with salt, pepper, and spices.

Pasta (Noodles)

Freshly made pasta noodles, *pasta fresca* or *fatta in casa,* are the finest pasta for lasagna. Other alternatives are available, especially when you don't have a lot of time. Check out your local pasta shop for fresh pasta noodles, usually sold in a variety of flavors.

Factory-made dried pasta noodles are available in most supermarkets. These usually have a traditional ruffled edge.

"No-boil" noodles are a nice way to prepare lasagna in a short time. Just be sure you have enough sauce to generously cover each layer of noodle, especially the top, so that the noodles will become tender during baking (the sauce and/or moisture from the filling will help to cook the noodles). With any store-bought pasta it's a good idea to try a few different brands and choose the one that you like best. I like the no-boil noodles. These are more like home-style noodles. To expedite the cooking and use less sauce, you can soak the no-boil sheets in hot tap water for ten to fifteen minutes, then drain on absorbent paper.

In most recipes, you can interchange fresh pasta sheets with soaked no-boil noodles, but it is important to remember that fresh pasta sheets are thinner. If you use them, you will have a shallow lasagna, or you can split the filling into thinner layers to accommodate more layers, thus yielding a taller lasagna. When substituting fresh pasta, just make a minor adjustment for the thinness.

No matter what type of noodles you are using, don't worry about irregular sizes or torn pieces of the noodles. They can be pieced together and will set up fine during the baking of the lasagna.

You can use a variety of other things in place of noodles for lasagna such as crepes, tortillas, egg roll wrappers, phyllo, and polenta.

There are also variations for flavored pastas, such as spinach and beet. Their flavors are subtle and the colors provide a striking presentation.

Prosciutto

This seasoned salt-cured ham has been air dried. It is usually available at most Italian delis. It's best when cut into very thin slices.

Tomatoes

In this collection of lasagna recipes we use a large variety of tomatoes. Tomatoes that are fresh from the garden like plum tomatoes and cherry tomatoes work well in a few of the quick sauces. Canned, peeled plum tomatoes should be a staple in every Italian pantry. Many times you can use whole peeled tomatoes and simply crush them by hand for a rustic slightly chunky sauce. If you like a smoother sauce, you can puree these tomatoes in a food processor. You can also use crushed tomatoes or petite diced tomatoes interchangeably for many of the recipes. Many excellent brands of canned tomatoes are available. My advice is simply to try a few and find the one that suits your own personal taste.

Tomato Paste

Tomato paste is tomatoes cooked and strained to highly concentrate the flavor. It will also help to thicken sauces. It is available in 6-ounce cans and also in smaller tubes, which make storage easier. You can use only as much as you need at one time.

EQUIPMENT TIPS

~~~~~~

Baking Dishes

Most of the baking dishes used in this book are of a size that is readily available and probably already exists in most kitchens. The 13 × 9 × 3-inch dish, the 8 × 8 × 2-inch, and the 11 × 7 × 1½-inch dishes are the most commonly used in this book. A glass baking dish is very common and handy when you want to check out how the sides and bottom of the lasagnas are looking. A ceramic dish works just as well and usually makes a better presentation when the lasagna goes from oven to table. Larger lasagnas use a large roasting pan, 18 × 13½ × 3 inches.

Many of the recipes can be adjusted to use different-size pans. Keep in mind that shallow pans will give you fewer layers of filling and a crustier top.

Disposable foil baking pans are not recommended for most situations but can certainly be used for what I call "meals on wheels." Often a casserole or lasagna becomes a gift to a family that is going through a difficult time. For these occasions, make lasagna in a disposable foil pan for giving. This eliminates anyone having to worry about returning what pan to what person. In this case, double the pans for extra strength.

Saucepans, Stockpots, and Skillets

Use heavy-gauge pans to prevent sauces from sticking to the bottom. This is especially important when the sauce cooks for a long period of time. The last thing you want is to labor intensively over an expensive meat ragu only to find it burnt and stuck to the bottom of your saucepan.

Many of the sauce recipes here are made or start out in a large skillet. A heavy-weight skillet with sturdy sides, 12 to 14 inches in diameter, works fine.

Spoons, Spatulas, Serving Utensils

Offset spatulas are ideal to remove slices and to spread fillings over noodles. Use a sharp straight-edge knife to cut and a flat spatula to remove pieces of lasagna from the baking dish or pan.

Tongs

These are ideal to maneuver long noodles in boiling water.

ESSENTIAL TIPS

Storing and Making Ahead

Many lasagnas can be prepared one day in advance. After assembly, cover with plastic wrap and refrigerate overnight. Be sure to let the lasagna come to room temperature before baking it.

How to Tell When Lasagna Is Done

Most lasagnas are baked initially with the top covered with foil. The foil is then removed for the remainder of the cooking time. You want the lasagna to be bubbly, well browned in spots, and hot in the center. For really large-size lasagnas I use a meat thermometer to be sure the internal temperature is 150°F.

Let the Lasagna Rest Before Serving

This is an important step. After baking, let the lasagna rest ten to fifteen minutes before cutting and serving. This will allow the sauces and fillings to set up and will give you a picture-perfect piece.

Individual Free-Form Lasagnas

Free-form lasagnas are not baked whole in a baking dish like most traditional lasagnas. They are simply noodles, filling, and sauce plated directly on a warmed plate and served individually. They are a nice way to redefine people's perception of lasagna and impress them with an individual portion instead of the usual family style.

For all free-form lasagnas, be sure the filling and sauce are hot to help to "cook" the pasta and make it tender. Warm the oven to 200°F. Store ovenproof plates in the oven until ready to portion lasagnas and serve, ten to fifteen minutes. Carefully remove and plate the lasagna. Store the stacked pastas in the oven until serving.

Lasagna

~~~~~~~~~

Essentials

Pasta (Noodles)

Fresh Egg Pasta

Spinach Pasta

Beet Pasta

Crepes

Whole Wheat Crepes

Fillings and Sauces

Basic Ricotta Filling

Béchamel Sauce (Salsa Besciamella)

Quick Tomato Sauce

Pesto Sauce

Mom's Sunday Sauce

PASTA (NOODLES)

~~~~~~~~~~

Delicate and delicious, these noodles are really worth the effort. When making dough for homemade pasta be aware that proportions are approximate. The texture of the dough will vary according to what size eggs you use, how humid the weather is, how you measure the flour, and the type of flour that you are using. It will also make a difference if you use a hand-mixing method, a mixer with a dough hook attachment, or a food processor to mix the dough. My husband, Edgar, likes to mix by hand or use the mixer with a dough hook. (He even rolls the dough with his grandmother's wooden rolling pin instead of using the pasta machine.) I tend to favor the food processor method. I think it yields more consistent dough and is a bit less messy.

Kneading is the key (knead for five minutes). Marcella Hazan says, "Press your thumb deep into the center of the dough. If it comes out clean, without sticky matter, you have enough flour." Also important in making pasta is to let the dough rest at room temperature before rolling it through the machine.

Fresh Egg Pasta

~~~~

1½ cups Italian 00 flour
   or all-purpose unbleached flour
Pinch of salt

2 eggs
2 tablespoons water
2 teaspoons extra virgin olive oil

MIXING BY HAND

On a lightly floured work surface, mound the flour and salt. Make a well in the center. In a small bowl, mix eggs, water, and olive oil. Pour egg mixture into well. With a fork gradually incorporate the egg mixture into the flour mixture. Knead until the dough is smooth and elastic, at least 5 minutes. Roll the dough into a ball, cover with plastic wrap, and let rest 15 to 20 minutes before rolling out.

FOOD PROCESSOR METHOD

Combine the flour and salt in a food processor fitted with a metal blade. Add the eggs, water, and olive oil. Pulse a few times to combine ingredients. Remove the dough from the food processor and knead until smooth and elastic, at least 5 minutes, dusting with additional flour if necessary. Roll the dough into a ball, cover with plastic wrap, and let rest at room temperature 15 to 20 minutes.

ROLLING AND CUTTING DOUGH WITH A PASTA MACHINE

Invest in a classic pasta-making machine. Several models are available, some with hand cranks and some with motors. This is the only way to get the pasta noodles delicate and thin. Most pasta machines have settings that range from #1 to #6, with #1 being the widest setting and #6 being the narrowest.

1. After letting the dough rest at room temperature, cut it into three equal pieces.
2. Lightly dust the pasta rollers, and crank each piece of dough through the widest setting twice.
3. Reset the rollers one size narrower. Run the pasta pieces through the rollers

twice on this setting, then cut the pasta pieces in half to make them easier to handle. This will give you six pieces of dough that are approximately 4 × 5 inches.

4. Roll pieces through the next two narrower settings (#3 and #4 settings) twice. Cut each piece of dough in half for easier handling. Run these pieces through the last two narrowest settings (#5 and #6), only one pass each setting.

5. Continue to roll on narrower settings until the desired thinness is reached. Number 5 or #6 produces a nice thin noodle that doesn't tear. You'll know it's thin enough if you can see your fingers through the dough, holding it from underneath. You should have approximately twelve pieces of dough about 3 to 4 inches wide by 10 to 12 inches long. Remember that if you cut the pasta into smaller pieces for easier handling, you will have a different number of pieces. If you are new to pasta making it's really more important that you are comfortable rolling pieces through rollers. They will be pieced together in the lasagna and it won't make a difference if they are not the ideal size.

6. Place the pasta sheets in a single layer on a lightly floured sheet pan. Dust the tops with flour and place a piece of parchment paper over the sheets. Continue to layer pasta sheets and parchment, lightly flouring between each layer. Cover pan tightly with plastic wrap. Use immediately or refrigerate overnight.

MAKES 12 PIECES, ABOUT 3 TO 4 INCHES × 10 TO 12 INCHES

ENOUGH FOR A 13 × 9 LASAGNA

How to Cook Pasta for Lasagna

FRESH PASTA:

Fresh pasta sheets do not take long to cook. Because they are so thin, a simple dip into boiling water will just about do it. The noodles will also continue to cook in the lasagna.

Bring a large pot of salted water to a boil. Place noodles three or four at a time into boiling water for 15 to 20 seconds. Remove pasta from the boiling water and transfer to an ice water bath with a strainer or a pair of tongs. This will immediately halt the cooking. Remove from ice water and drain on absorbent paper.

DRIED PASTA SHEETS:

Bring a large pot of salted water to a boil. Cook pasta al dente, a little less than the manufacturer's directions recommend. The noodles will cook again in the lasagna. Drain on absorbent paper.

NO-BOIL NOODLES:

Last-minute lasagna is now a possibility. The key is having enough moisture and sauce to cook the noodles as the lasagna bakes. Be sure you have a generous amount of sauce if using no-boil noodles straight from the box. Some recipes use a shortcut for the no-boil noodles that my friend and great chef Sally Maraventano taught me. Fill a large bowl with hot tap water. Soak the noodles for 10 to 15 minutes. Drain on absorbent paper. They are now ready to use.

Spinach Pasta

~~~~~~

Use a piece of cheesecloth or paper towel to drain and squeeze all the excess water out of thawed spinach. Chopping it finely in a food processor will make the spinach blend more uniformly when mixing the pasta dough. Otherwise, it will look like a speckled herb pasta, not a rich green spinach pasta.

½ cup frozen spinach, thawed, excess liquid squeezed out, and finely chopped in a food processor

1½ cups Italian 00 flour or all-purpose unbleached flour

Pinch of salt

2 eggs

1 tablespoon water

2 teaspoons extra virgin olive oil

Follow previous directions for mixing, rolling, and cutting pasta sheets. Mix spinach in with flour.

MAKES 12 PIECES,
ABOUT 4 INCHES WIDE × 12 INCHES LONG

Whole Wheat Pasta

~~~

This hearty pasta can used in just about any lasagna. I like it with a pungent sauce like Puttanesca (page 56), Spicy Tomato Sauce (page 64), or a flavorful meat ragu.

1½ cups whole wheat flour
   (medium grade)
¼ cup all-purpose flour
Pinch of salt

2 eggs
2 tablespoons water
1 teaspoon extra virgin olive oil

Follow previous directions for mixing, rolling, and cutting pasta sheets.

MAKES 12 PIECES,
ABOUT 4 INCHES WIDE × 14 INCHES LONG

Beet Pasta

~~~~~~

Pureed beets add a fantastic color to homemade pasta sheets. This pasta stars in our Beet Lasagna with Creamy Gorgonzola Sauce (page 108), but you can use it simply layered with pecorino and béchamel as well. To roast the beets, wrap washed beets in aluminum foil and bake for 1 to 1½ hours until fork tender. Let cool slightly, then pull off skin. Process in food processor until smooth.

½ cup pureed roasted beets (about 1 medium beet)

2 cups Italian 00 flour or all-purpose unbleached flour

Pinch of salt

2 eggs

2 teaspoons extra virgin olive oil

Follow previous directions for mixing, rolling, and cutting pasta sheets. Mix beets in with flour.

MAKES 12 PIECES,
ABOUT 3 INCHES WIDE × 12 INCHES LONG

CREPES

~~~~~

Using crepes instead of noodles is another great way to make lasagna.

Don't worry about trying to fit round crepes in a square pan. Just slightly overlap and layer the lasagna and it will all fit in and set up while it's baking.

Basic Crepes

~~~~~

These are my mom's manicotti crepes that I also use as a tender lasagna noodle. They can be interchanged with fresh pasta noodles in most recipes. This batch can be easily doubled so you can freeze crepes ahead of time.

3 eggs
1 cup water

1 cup all-purpose flour
Pinch of salt

1. In an electric mixer, combine the eggs and water. Mix until well blended. Gradually add the flour and salt. Mix until smooth. Use immediately or refrigerate in an airtight container. (Batter can be made one day in advance.)

2. Heat a 7-inch nonstick skillet over medium-high heat. Ladle a scant ½ cup of batter into the heated skillet. Roll pan around so that batter can cover the surface of the pan. Cook the crepe until the bottom is light brown. Carefully use a spatula to turn the crepe over and continue cooking the underside until light brown as well.

3. Use the crepes immediately, or store in refrigerator or freezer. To store, lay crepes on top of parchment paper. Layer crepes with parchment in between. Place in heavy-duty plastic bag.

MAKES 12 CREPES

Whole Wheat Crepes

~~~

These tasty crepes add a nice texture and color to your lasagnas. They are delicious in our Autumn Pancetta and Porcini Lasagna (page 83) but can be used in any of the other recipes as well.

3 eggs
1 cup water
½ cup all-purpose flour

½ cup whole wheat flour
Pinch of salt

In an electric mixer, combine the eggs and water. Mix until well blended. Gradually add both flours and salt. Mix until smooth. Use immediately or store in refrigerator in an airtight container. (Batter can be made one day in advance.) Cook and store like basic crepes.

MAKES 10 TO 12 CREPES

FILLINGS AND SAUCES

~~~~~

Fillings for lasagna do not need to be cheesy and heavy. Rather, a creamy béchamel or a delicate ricotta-based filling is the perfect way to accompany noodles and a home-made sauce.

Sauce for lasagnas can be a creamy béchamel, a light pomodoro (tomato), or a hearty meat ragu. (A ragu is typically a flavorful meat sauce.)

Basic Ricotta Filling

~~~~~

2 eggs
1 pound ricotta
1 pound mozzarella, cubed

½ cup grated pecorino Romano
½ cup chopped parsley
Salt and pepper

In a mixing bowl, whisk eggs until blended. Add ricotta, mozzarella, pecornio, parsley, and salt and pepper. Refrigerate in an airtight container.

MAKES ABOUT 3 CUPS

Béchamel Sauce
(*Salsa Besciamella*)

〜〜〜

This classic white sauce is made from butter, flour, and milk. Almost equal parts of these ingredients are used to create this creamy filling for lasagna. It acts as an ingredient binder and adds a delicate balance to many of the flavorful meat ragus used in classic lasagna preparation. The key to success when making béchamel is easy: never let the butter cook until it browns, or the sauce will have a burnt taste. Heating the milk in a separate pan really helps to create a smooth thick sauce. Add the milk slowly, whisking constantly to avoid lumps. Below is the master recipe with variations for different amounts depending on the amount of sauce you need. Use unsalted butter for the freshest flavor.

2-Cup Béchamel Sauce
2 cups milk
3 tablespoons unsalted butter
3 tablespoons all-purpose flour
Salt and pepper

3-Cup Béchamel Sauce
3 cups milk
4 tablespoons (½ stick) unsalted butter
¼ cup all-purpose flour
Salt and pepper

4-Cup Béchamel Sauce
4 cups milk
5 tablespoons unsalted butter
5 tablespoons all-purpose flour
Salt and pepper

10-Cup Béchamel Sauce
10 cups milk
12 tablespoons (1½ sticks) butter
½ cup all-purpose flour
Salt and pepper

BÉCHAMEL MASTER RECIPE

1. In a saucepan, heat the milk over low heat just until small bubbles come to the surface. Remove the pan from direct heat, cover, and keep warm.

2. In a separate saucepan over medium heat, melt butter.

3. Whisk the flour into the butter and continue to whisk for 1 minute.

4. Gradually whisk in the warmed milk; bring to a simmer, and whisk frequently until thickened, 4 to 5 minutes for a small batch, 6 to 8 for a larger batch.

5. Remove from the heat. Stir in salt and pepper. To prevent a skin from forming on top of the sauce, either whisk occasionally as the sauce cools or place a piece of plastic wrap directly on top of the surface of the sauce. Use the béchamel immediately or cool to room temperature. Pour into an airtight container and refrigerate overnight. Reheat sauce, stirring, over low heat before assembling lasagna.

Quick Tomato Sauce

~~~~~

3 tablespoons extra virgin olive oil
2 garlic cloves, minced
One 35-ounce can peeled whole
    tomatoes, crushed by hand,
    with juice

Salt and pepper
3 fresh basil leaves, torn into large
    pieces

In a large skillet, heat the olive oil over medium-high heat. Add garlic and cook until just beginning to brown, 30 to 40 seconds. Add tomatoes and salt and pepper. Bring to a boil. Reduce heat to low and simmer uncovered for about 20 to 25 minutes until thickened. Stir in the basil.

Use immediately or store in an airtight container, refrigerated, 3 to 4 days or frozen for up to 3 weeks. To thaw, refrigerate sauce overnight. Reheat sauce on low until thawed.

MAKES 4 CUPS

Pesto Sauce

～～～

Nothing defines summer like fresh bright green basil pesto. This classic recipe uses pine nuts and the finest olive oil. You can make a batch or two with your summer crop and freeze for later use. If you are freezing it, omit the cheese; add it when you thaw the pesto for a fresher taste.

2 cups basil leaves, washed and
    dried
2 tablespoons pine nuts
2 garlic cloves

Salt and pepper
½ cup grated pecorino Romano
¾ cup extra virgin olive oil

In a food processor, combine the basil leaves, pine nuts, garlic, salt and pepper, and pecorino. Pulse until crushed. Pour olive oil through the top of the food processor in a steady stream and mix until blended. Use immediately or refrigerate overnight in an airtight container. Freeze for I to 2 weeks. Thaw at room temperature.

MAKES 1 CUP

Mom's Sunday Sauce

~~~~~~

This is my mom's classic meat sauce. It's loaded with meatballs, pork ribs, brasciole (beef rolls), and flavor. This sauce is a labor of love and makes a generous 14 cups of sauce, so you can freeze some for later use. Here are some tips for getting the best results:

Because this sauce cooks for a long time, use a heavy saucepan to be sure the bottom of the sauce doesn't burn. The pan must be large enough to accommodate all the meat and tomatoes.

Freeze the sauce in an airtight container, portioning a variety of meat in each container. Thaw frozen sauce overnight in the refrigerator.

Meatballs

1½ pounds ground beef (80 percent
    lean, 20 percent fat)
½ cup fresh bread crumbs
1 egg

2 tablespoons chopped parsley
½ cup grated pecorino Romano
Salt and pepper

1. In a medium mixing bowl combine all ingredients. Mix until incorporated.
2. Roll the meat mixture into balls slightly larger than golf balls. Set aside.

MAKES ABOUT 16 MEATBALLS

Brasciole

These garlic- and cheese-stuffed beef rolls add a great flavor to the meat sauce.

¾ pound shoulder steak (chuck),
    sliced into 4 thin pieces
Salt and pepper
4 garlic cloves, minced

2 teaspoons chopped parsley
2 tablespoons grated pecorino
    Romano

1. Trim any excess fat from edges of meat. Place meat between two pieces of wax paper. Pound each piece of steak until it's about ¼ inch thick.

2. Season each piece of meat with salt and pepper. Rub garlic, parsley, and cheese onto meat.

3. Starting at the short end, roll meat jelly-roll fashion. Tie each roll into a small package, using three pieces of string for each roll. Tie the first piece of string around the middle of the roll and knot it. Then tie and knot one piece of string close to each end so that the seasoning stays inside. Don't fret if some of it comes out. It will flavor the sauce. The tying is to keep the majority of the seasoning inside.

MAKES 4 ROLLS

Sunday Sauce

¼ cup olive oil
Meatballs (page 18)
Brasciole (page 18)
1 pound sweet Italian sausage
2 pounds country-style pork ribs
   with bones (about 4 pieces)

1 large onion, diced
2 garlic cloves, minced
Three 35-ounce cans peeled
   tomatoes, crushed by hand
Salt and pepper
One 6-ounce can tomato paste

1. In a large heavy saucepan, heat the olive oil over medium-high heat. Add the meatballs and brown all over, turning gently.

2. Remove meatballs with slotted spoon and set aside.

3. To the same pan, add the brasciole. Brown all over, about 5 minutes. Remove with a slotted spoon and set aside.

4. To the same pan, add the sausage and brown all over. Remove and set aside. Repeat, browning with ribs. Set aside.

5. To the same pan, add onion. Cook, stirring frequently with a wooden spoon, for about 3 minutes.

6. Add garlic. Cook for 1 minute.

7. Add the tomatoes and tomato paste and bring to a boil. Using a wooden spoon,

scrape up any browned bits from the bottom of the pan. Bring to a boil over medium-high heat. Reduce heat to low and simmer, uncovered, stirring occasionally, for about 2½ hours. Season with salt and pepper.

8. Store in an airtight container. Refrigerate 3 to 4 days or freeze 2 to 3 weeks. Thaw in refrigerator overnight, then place over low heat to reheat.

MAKES 14 CUPS

Starters

Crostini

White Bean Spread

Creamy Artichoke Spread

Fig and Goat Cheese Spread

Crispy Polenta and Pesto Bites

Zucchini Carpaccio with Lemon Vinaigrette

Garlic Bread

In most cases your oven will be busy baking lasagna, so here are a few ideas for appetizers, most of which don't require oven time. These tasty starters allow you enough time to mingle with guests while dinner cooks. Many times I simply prepare an antipasto of Italian specialties. Many gourmet food stores have a good selection of cured meats (salumi), cheeses, fresh fruit, olives, and pickled vegetables (eggplant, peppers, mushrooms). An assortment of any of these items can be the perfect way to start a meal.

Crostini

~~~~~

Crostini are tiny bites of toast, drizzled with olive oil and topped with a variety of tasty spreads. You can also use crackers, bread sticks, or toasted pitas for these spreads. Try a White Bean Spread, (page 25), Creamy Artichoke Spread (page 25), or Fig and Goat Cheese Spread (page 26).

One 9-ounce baguette, diagonally
   sliced into ¼-inch slices

2 tablespoons extra virgin olive oil
Salt

1. Preheat the broiler.
2. Place slices of baguette on a cookie sheet in a single layer. Drizzle with olive oil and sprinkle with salt.
3. Broil for 1 to 2 minutes until golden brown. Let cool.
4. Top with desired topping. Store unused toasts in an airtight container.

MAKES ABOUT 20 SLICES

White Bean Spread

~~~

One 15-ounce can white cannellini
    beans, rinsed and drained
2 garlic cloves

Salt and pepper
3 basil leaves
¼ cup extra virgin olive oil

1. Place the beans, garlic, salt and pepper, and basil in a food processor. Pulse until smooth.

2. Add olive oil in a steady stream. Mix until incorporated. (Can be made 2 to 3 days in advance. Refrigerate in an airtight container.)

MAKES 1½ CUPS

Creamy Artichoke Spread

~~~

One 14-ounce can artichoke hearts,
    drained
3 tablespoons mayonnaise
1 garlic clove
2 tablespoons lemon juice

2 tablespoons parsley
2 tablespoons grated pecorino
    Romano
½ teaspoon salt
¼ teaspoon pepper

1. Place all the ingredients in a food processor. Pulse until mixed but still slightly chunky. (Can be made 1 to 2 days in advance. Refrigerate in an airtight container.)

MAKES 1 CUP

Fig and Goat Cheese Spread

~~~

3 ounces goat cheese

3 ounces cream cheese

8 dried figs

1 teaspoon fresh thyme

Place all the ingredients in a food processor. Pulse until smooth. (Can be prepared 3 to 4 days in advance. Refrigerate in an airtight container.)

MAKES 1 CUP

Crispy Polenta with Pesto Bites

～～～

For this easy, tasty appetizer you can purchase prepared polenta or make instant polenta. Making the pesto ahead of time makes these snacks a snap to prepare.

Instant Polenta

1 quart water
1 cup instant polenta

¼ cup grated pecorino Romano

1. In a large pan, bring the water to a boil.
2. Whisk in polenta gradually. Continue to whisk until polenta is thickened.
3. Remove from heat. Stir in pecorino.
4. Pour into a greased 13 × 9 × 3-inch pan. Cool, then cover and refrigerate overnight. (Polenta can be made 2 or 3 days in advance.)

Pesto Bites

¼ cup extra virgin olive oil
Prepared polenta, cut into 1-inch
   squares or circles
Pesto Sauce (page 17)

or Sun-Dried Tomato Pesto (page
   84)
or Black Olive Pesto (page 132)

In a large skillet, heat olive oil over medium-high heat. Add polenta squares. Cook for 2 to 3 minutes on each side until lightly browned and crisp. Top with desired pesto. Serve warm or at room temperature.

MAKES 60 POLENTA SQUARES

Zucchini Carpaccio with Lemon Vinaigrette

~~~

Use a mandoline to shave this farm-fresh summer squash into thin slices. Dress them with the best quality olive oil and shaved Parmesan for an easy appetizer. Try this vinaigrette on roasted asparagus, too.

Lemon Vinaigrette
¼ cup balsamic vinegar
2 tablespoons lemon juice
½ teaspoon Dijon mustard
1 garlic clove, minced
¾ cup extra virgin olive oil
Salt and pepper

Carpaccio
3 medium zucchini, shaved into thin slices
Parmigiano-Reggiano shavings

1. In a small bowl, whisk all dressing ingredients together until blended. Use immediately or store, refrigerated, in an airtight container.
2. Pour over shaved zucchini. Serve with Parmesan shavings.

MAKES 6 SERVINGS

Garlic Bread

This is another of my mom's specialties. Any leftover bread makes really good croutons. You can use any leftovers in Panzanella (page 39).

Garlic Butter
10 tablespoons butter, softened
3 garlic cloves, minced
Salt and pepper
2 tablespoons chopped parsley

Two 9-ounce baguettes, sliced in half
   horizontally

1. Preheat broiler.
2. Mix all ingredients for garlic butter. Stir until blended.
3. Spread on bread. Place bread on a cookie sheet. Broil until bread is toasted, 2 to 5 minutes. Slice into serving pieces and serve immediately.

MAKES 4 SERVINGS

Salads and

Dressings

Caesar Salad with Caesar Dressing

Insalata Caprese

Jerry's Pink Grapefruit Caprese

Fennel and Arugula Salad

Panzanella

House Salad

Mom's Creamy Italian Dressing

Fresh salad is a natural companion to any of the lasagnas. Here are a few suggestions—my favorite homemade Caesar, crisp fennel and arugula, or classic Caprese salad. Be sure to use the freshest well-washed ingredients for all of your salads.

Caesar Salad with Caesar Dressing

~~~

This classic salad is loaded with garlic and accented with fresh croutons and shaved Parmesan. The dressing is easy to prepare in the food processor, and using anchovy paste gives great flavor without the mess of using the actual fish.

4 hearts romaine lettuce, washed, drained, and torn into pieces
Grated Parmesan

Garlic Croutons
Half a day-old baguette
3 tablespoons olive oil
2 garlic cloves, minced

Caesar Dressing
2 garlic cloves
1 egg (see Note, page 35)
¼ cup grated Parmesan
1 teaspoon anchovy paste
2 tablespoons lemon juice
¼ cup balsamic vinegar
1 cup olive oil

1. Place the lettuce in a large bowl. Set aside.
2. For the croutons, cut the bread into cubes. Heat the olive oil in a large skillet. Add the garlic. Add bread cubes and stir until toasted, 3 to 5 minutes. Add to lettuce. (Use croutons immediately or store in an airtight container.)
3. Prepare the dressing. In a food processor, combine all ingredients except the olive oil. Pulse until smooth.
4. Add olive oil slowly in a stream. Mix until blended. (Use immediately or refrigerate 1 to 2 days.)
5. Pour dressing over greens and croutons and toss. Top with additional Parmesan.

SERVES 4

A Note on Egg Safety

If you'd rather not use a raw egg in the dressing, you can add a coddled egg to the dressing. To coddle eggs, place a room-temperature egg in simmering water for 1 to 2 minutes. Remove from water, crack open, and whisk into dressing.

Microwave: Crack egg into a small glass bowl. Place bowl in microwave and heat for 12 to 15 seconds. Transfer egg to ice water to stop cooking. Whisk into dressing.

Insalata Caprese

~~~~~

This classic salad combines the best mozzarella with the ripest tomatoes and basil.

2 ripe medium tomatoes, sliced
8 ounces fresh mozzarella
6 to 8 basil leaves

Sea salt and freshly ground pepper
¼ cup extra virgin olive oil

1. On a serving plate arrange slices of tomatoes, mozzarella, and basil, slightly overlapping.

2. Season with salt and pepper. Drizzle with olive oil. Serve at room temperature.

SERVES 4

Jerry's Pink Grapefruit Caprese

~~~

The recipe for this refreshing salad comes from one of my favorite restaurants, The Woodward House in Bethlehem, Connecticut. Chef Jerry Reveron shares this version of Caprese that stars mozzarella di bufala (buffalo mozzarella), pink grapefruit, and pomegranate seeds. To make the balsamic reduction, simmer ½ cup balsamic vinegar until syrupy and reduced to just under ¼ cup.

1 grapefruit, peeled, cut into slices
   about ⅛ inch thick
8 ounces mozzarella di bufala,
   sliced ⅛ inch thick
Salt

2 tablespoons pomegranate seeds
¼ cup extra virgin olive oil
¼ cup balsamic reduction (see
   headnote)

1. On a serving plate, arrange slices of grapefruit and mozzarella, slightly overlapping.

2. Season with salt. Sprinkle with pomegranate seeds. Drizzle with olive oil and balsamic reduction.

SERVES 4

Fennel and Arugula Salad

~~~

This flavorful salad has the pungent taste of fennel complemented by fresh juicy oranges and toasted almonds.

10 ounces baby arugula
1 medium fennel bulb, trimmed and
   thinly sliced
2 oranges, peeled and sliced

½ cup sliced almonds, toasted
Salt
½ cup olive oil
6 tablespoons fresh lemon juice

In a medium mixing bowl combine arugula, fennel, oranges, and almonds. Season with salt. Drizzle with olive oil and lemon juice. Toss to coat.

SERVES 4

Panzanella

~~~

This classic Tuscan bread salad is a combination of ripe tomatoes, cucumbers, red onion, and day-old bread. To this classic I like to add some chickpeas, too.

2 cucumbers, peeled and sliced
2 ripe tomatoes, cut into ½-inch
   pieces
½ red onion, cut into ½-inch slices
One 15-ounce can chickpeas, rinsed
   and drained

Half a day-old baguette, cut into
   ½-inch pieces
¼ cup extra virgin olive oil
3 tablespoons balsamic vinegar
Sea salt and pepper
½ teaspoon chopped fresh oregano

1. In a medium bowl, combine cucumbers, tomatoes, red onion, chickpeas, and bread. Drizzle with extra virgin olive oil and vinegar.

2. Season with salt, pepper, and oregano. Toss. Let sit at room temperature 15 to 20 minutes to soften the bread.

SERVES 4

House Salad

This has become my house salad. Add cooked bacon or pancetta bits for added flavor. In fall or winter, I sometimes omit the avocado and apple and substitute a pear and ½ cup crumbled Gorgonzola cheese, and a handful of walnuts.

1 head butter lettuce, washed, drained, and torn into pieces

1 Granny Smith apple, peeled, cored, and sliced

½ small red onion, chopped

1 avocado, cut into ½-inch pieces

Salt and pepper

¼ cup olive oil

3 tablespoons apple cider vinegar

In a medium bowl, combine lettuce, apple, onion, and avocado. Season with salt and pepper. Toss with olive oil and vinegar.

SERVES 4

Mom's Creamy Italian Dressing

~~~

This dressing was always a special treat when we were growing up. Mom would pour this over her famous house salad of greens, cucumbers, red onions, black olives, and chopped celery.

1 cup mayonnaise
½ small onion
2 tablespoons red wine vinegar
1 tablespoon sugar

¼ teaspoon salt
Pinch of pepper
½ teaspoon chopped fresh oregano

1. Place all ingredients in a blender or food processor. Blend until smooth.
2. Refrigerate dressing in an airtight container until using. (Can be made 2 to 3 days in advance.)

MAKES 1¼ CUPS

Classic

Lasagnas

Pomodoro Lasagna 🌿

Lasagna Bolognese

Italian-American Lasagna

"Tutti Famiglia" Lasagna

Winnie's Chicken Sauce Lasagna

Sausage and Pepper Lasagna

Puttanesca Lasagna

Arugula and Prosciutto Lasagna

Lasagne Quattro Stagione

Sausage Mushroom Lasagna
with Pink Sauce

Sausage and Broccoli Rabe Lasagna
with Spicy Tomato Sauce

Lazy Carbonara Penne for a Crowd

"Lazy Lasagna" with Vodka Sauce 🌿

Paglia e Fieno (Straw and Hay)
Lasagna

Lasagna Quattro Formaggi 🌿

Carnevale Lasagna

Lasagna alla Norma 🌿

Winter Lasagna

Lasagna Primavera 🌿

Late Summer Lasagna 🌿

Autumn Pancetta and Porcini Lasagna

Double Pesto Lasagna 🌿

Classic Vegetarian Lasagna 🌿

Tortellini Lasagna

Lasagna Caprese 🌿

🌿 vegetarian

Pomodoro Lasagna

These bright and colorful individual lasagnas are simple to prepare and impressive to serve. The egg pasta layers are light and delicate like hankerchiefs. They are perfect summer "no-bake" lasagnas. Quick-cooking the garden tomatoes gives the sauce its fresh flavor in the Bella Napoli style, literally in the style of "beautiful Naples." Napoletanos are famous for serving their pasta with a dollop of fresh ricotta on the side.

Sauce
10 ounces red and 10 ounces yellow
    grape tomatoes, cut in half
Salt and pepper
½ cup extra virgin olive oil
2 tablespoons chopped basil
2 tablespoons chopped parsley

Noodles
8 pieces of fresh pasta (page 4),
    cooked according to directions
    on page 6, and cut in half
Parmigiano-Reggiano shavings
1 cup ricotta

PREPARE SAUCE

1. In a small bowl, combine tomatoes and salt and pepper and toss.

2. In a medium skillet, heat olive oil over medium-high heat. Add tomatoes. Sauté for 1 minute. Reduce heat and simmer for 15 to 20 minutes.

3. Add basil and parsley.

LAYER BY LAYER ASSEMBLY

4. Place one piece of pasta on a small plate. Top with tomato mixture.

5. Top with another piece of pasta.

6. Continue to layer sauce and pasta, using four layers of noodles for each individual lasagna. Top with a few tomatoes and a generous shaving of Parmesan. Serve with a dollop of ricotta on the side.

SERVES 4

Lasagna Bolognese

~~~~~~~~

This is the traditional original lasagna, first cooked in Bologna. It's a hearty dish made of multiple layerings of regular and spinach noodles, filled with rich Bolognese sauce and creamy béchamel.

Use a food processor to chop the onions, celery, and carrots. Look for meat that is not too lean. You'll want some fat from the meat to add flavor to the sauce.

The sauce recipe can be easily doubled for a large lasagna, or frozen for later use.

Bolognese Sauce
¼ cup extra virgin olive oil
1 cup chopped onion
½ cup chopped celery
½ cup chopped carrots
1½ pounds ground beef
Salt and pepper
Two 35-ounce cans peeled tomatoes,
   crushed by hand
6 ounces tomato paste

Filling
3-Cup Béchamel Sauce (page 14)
1 cup grated pecorino Romano, plus
   some for serving

Noodles
Fresh Egg Pasta (page 4), cooked
   according to directions on page 6
Spinach Pasta (page 7)

PREPARE SAUCE

1. In a large skillet, heat olive oil over medium heat.

2. Add onion, celery, and carrots. Cook until tender, but not brown, about 10 minutes.

3. Add the beef. Using a wooden spoon, break up bits of meat and stir occasionally. Cook until meat is almost cooked through, 10 to 15 minutes. Season with salt and pepper.

4. Add tomatoes and tomato paste. Bring to a boil.

5. Reduce heat to low and simmer for 2 hours, uncovered, stirring occasionally.

6. Preheat oven to 375°F.

7. Spray a 13×9×3-inch baking dish with nonstick cooking spray.

8. Spread a layer of Bolognese Sauce on the bottom of the dish. Cover with egg noodles, slightly overlapping.

9. For the filling, spread a layer of Béchamel Sauce over the noodles and sprinkle with pecorino.

10. Top with spinach noodles.

11. Continue to layer in the following order until you have run out of noodles, reserving some of both sauces:

Bolognese Sauce

Pecorino

Egg noodles

Béchamel Sauce

Spinach noodles

Bolognese Sauce

Pecorino

Egg noodles

12. Top with remaining Béchamel Sauce and pecorino. Reserve the remaining Bolognese Sauce for serving. *Advance prep completed.* (The lasagna can be made one day in advance to this step. Cover and refrigerate overnight. Let lasagna come to room temperature before baking.)

BAKING

13. Cover with foil and bake for 40 to 50 minutes. Remove foil and continue to bake for an additional 10 to 15 minutes. Remove from the oven. Let rest 10 to 15 minutes until serving. Serve with additional Bolognese Sauce and pecorino.

SERVES 6 TO 8

Italian-American Lasagna

~~~~~

This classic lasagna is the kind that defines lasagna in the USA: ruffle-edged noodles, creamy ricotta and mozzarella filling, and a rich tomato sauce. Here we have a few options for sauce, depending on your personal preference. My mom always used her robust meat-laden Sunday sauce, but the lasagna is still delicious with another sauce such as Chicken Sauce, Bolognese Sauce, or a meat-free sauce like Quick Tomato Sauce or Vodka Sauce.

Sauce

Quick Tomato Sauce (page 16)
or Vodka Sauce (page 68)
or half of recipe Mom's Sunday
    Sauce (page 18)
or Chicken Sauce (page 52)
or Bolognese Sauce (page 46)

Classic Cheese Filling

2 eggs
1 pound whole milk ricotta
2 cups cubed mozzarella, plus 2 cups
    shredded
½ cup grated pecorino Romano, plus
    some for serving
¼ cup chopped parsley
Salt and pepper

Noodles

10 ruffle-edged (dried) noodles,
    boiled until al dente and drained

PREPARE FILLING

1. In a medium mixing bowl, whisk eggs until blended. Add ricotta, cubed mozzarella, pecorino Romano, parsley, and salt and pepper. Mix until blended.

2. Preheat oven to 375°F.

3. Spray a 13×9×3-inch baking dish with nonstick cooking spray.

LAYER BY LAYER ASSEMBLY

4. Spread a layer of sauce on the bottom of the dish. Top with three to four noodles, slightly overlapping.

5. Dot one-third of the cheese filling on top of the noodles. Spread with more sauce and top with noodles.

6. Repeat layers until all noodles and filling are used up.

7. Cover top layer of noodles with a generous amount of sauce. Top with shredded mozzarella. *Advance prep completed.* (Can be assembled one day in advance. Cover and refrigerate overnight. Let lasagna come to room temperature before baking.)

BAKING

8. Cover with foil and bake for 40 to 45 minutes. Remove foil and continue to bake for an additional 10 to 15 minutes. Remove from the oven. Let rest 10 to 15 minutes before serving. Serve with additional pecorino.

SERVES 6

"Tutti Famiglia" Lasagna

~~~~~~

This oversize lasagna is perfect for large family gatherings. I have nicknamed it "mega-sagna" because it will feed twenty guests. A combination of Bolognese Sauce and Italian-American filling is sure to please the whole crowd. Because it's bigger than the average lasagna, it will take a bit longer to cook.

Sauce

2 recipes Bolognese Sauce (page 46)

Italian-American Cheese Filling

2 eggs

2 pounds whole milk ricotta

2 pounds mozzarella, cubed

½ cup grated pecorino Romano, plus some for serving

½ cup grated Parmesan

1 cup chopped parsley

Salt and pepper

Noodles

64 no-boil noodles, soaked in hot tap water for 10 to 15 minutes and drained

or

48 Crepes (page 10)

FOR THE FILLING

1. In a large mixing bowl whisk eggs until blended. Add ricotta, mozzarella, pecorino, Parmesan, and parsley. Season with salt and pepper. Mix until blended.

2. Preheat oven to 375°F.

3. Spray an 18 × 13½ × 3-inch roasting pan with nonstick cooking spray.

LAYER BY LAYER ASSEMBLY

4. Spread a layer of sauce on the bottom of the pan. Top with a layer of noodles, slightly overlapping.

5. Dot with cheese filling. Spread a layer of sauce and top with noodles.

6. Repeat layers until all noodles and filling are used up.

7. Cover top noodles with a generous amount of sauce, reserving some sauce for serving. *Advanced prep completed.* (Can be assembled one day in advance. Cover and refrigerate overnight. Let lasagna come to room temperature before baking.)

BAKING

8. Cover top of lasagna with foil and bake for 50 to 60 minutes. Remove foil and continue to bake for an additional 20 to 30 minutes. Remove from the oven.

9. Let lasagna rest for 15 to 20 minutes before serving. Serve with additional sauce and pecorino.

SERVES 20

Make crepes ahead and freeze to save time. See page 11 for instructions.

Winnie's Chicken Sauce Lasagna

〜〜〜

My husband Edgar's Sicilian grandmother, Vincenza aka "Winnie," taught me how to make this hearty chicken ragu. I've made it the focus of this lasagna, in her honor. Paired with a creamy béchamel or a classic cheese filling, it makes a perfect Sunday afternoon meal.

Chicken Sauce

2 tablespoons extra virgin olive oil
Salt and pepper
2 pounds skinless chicken thighs,
 with bone (about 6 pieces)
1½ pounds skinless chicken breasts,
 with bone (about 2 pieces)
¾ cup diced onion
2 garlic cloves, minced
¼ cup minced parsley
½ cup white wine
Two 35-ounce cans peeled tomatoes,
 crushed by hand, liquid reserved

Filling

Classic Cheese Filling (page 48) or
3-cup Béchamel Sauce (page 14)
½ cup grated pecorino Romano, plus
 some for serving

Noodles

16 no-boil noodles, soaked in hot tap
 water for 10 to 15 minutes and
 drained

PREPARE SAUCE

1. In a large Dutch oven or saucepan, heat olive oil over medium-high heat. Salt and pepper the chicken.

2. Working in batches, brown chicken all over. Remove chicken pieces. Set aside.

3. Add onion and garlic to pan. Cook for 1 to 2 minutes.

4. Add parsley and wine. Scrape up any browned bits from the bottom of the pan.

5. Add tomatoes with their liquid.

6. Return chicken to pan. Bring to a boil. Reduce heat and simmer, uncovered, until chicken is tender, about 3 hours.

7. Remove chicken from the sauce. Using two forks, take the meat off the bones

and discard all bones and fat. Return the meat to the sauce. (Sauce can be made 1 to 2 days in advance. Cover and refrigerate, or store in an airtight container and freeze for 2 weeks.)

8. Preheat oven to 375°F.

9. Spray a 13 × 9 × 3-inch baking dish with nonstick cooking spray.

LAYER BY LAYER ASSEMBLY

10. Spread a layer of chicken sauce on the bottom of the dish. Top with four noodles, slightly overlapping.

11. Dot the noodles with one-third of the cheese filling (or top with Béchamel Sauce, page 14). Spread a layer of chicken sauce. Repeat layering until noodles and filling are used up—four layers of noodles and three of the filling.

13. Cover top noodles with a generous amount of chicken sauce. Sprinkle with pecorino, reserving some for serving. *Advance prep completed.* (Can be prepared one day in advance. Cover and refrigerate overnight. Let lasagna come to room temperature before baking.)

BAKING

14. Cover with foil and bake for 45 to 55 minutes. Remove foil and continue to bake for an additional 10 to 15 minutes. Remove from the oven. Let rest 10 to 15 minutes before serving. Serve with additional pecorino.

SERVES 6

Sausage and Pepper Lasagna

~~~

Two popular Italian flavor favorites combine to make this hearty main dish lasagna. It makes a great weekday supper paired with a green salad and crusty bread.

Sauce
3 tablespoons extra virgin olive oil
1 medium onion, chopped
1 large green bell pepper, diced
1 pound sweet Italian sausage,
   casings removed
One 28-ounce can peeled tomatoes,
   crushed by hand, liquid reserved
Salt and pepper

Filling
1½ cups shredded mozzarella
½ cup grated pecorino Romano, plus
   some for serving

Noodles
8 no-boil noodles, soaked in hot tap
   water for 10 to 15 minutes and
   drained

PREPARE SAUCE

1. In a large skillet, heat olive oil over medium-high heat. Add onion and green pepper and cook, stirring occasionally, until tender, about 5 minutes.

2. Add sausage and cook, breaking up bits of sausage with wooden spoon. Cook until sausage is cooked all the way through.

3. Add tomatoes with their liquid. Add salt and pepper. Bring to a boil. Reduce heat and simmer for 20 minutes, uncovered, until sauce is thickened.

4. Preheat oven to 375°F.

5. Spray an 8 × 8 × 2-inch baking dish with nonstick cooking spray.

LAYER BY LAYER ASSEMBLY

6. Spread a layer of sauce on the bottom of the dish. Top with two noodles, slightly overlapping.

7. For the filling, combine the cheeses and sprinkle the noodles with one-third of the filling. Top with a layer of sauce, and then two additional noodles.

8. Repeat another layer.

9. Cover top noodles with a generous layer of sauce. *Advance prep completed.* (Can be made one day in advance. Cover and refrigerate overnight. Let come to room temperature before baking.)

BAKING

10. Cover with foil and bake for 40 to 45 minutes. Remove foil and continue to bake for 10 to 15 minutes. Remove from the oven. Let rest 10 to 15 minutes before serving. Serve with additional pecorino.

SERVES 4 TO 6

Puttanesca Lasagna

～～～

This flavorful lasagna, studded with olives, capers, and tomato uses the classic Puttanesca Sauce. This sauce has had a reputation for being the meal of choice for prostitutes to prepare for their clients. Other folklore points to a similar rumor that the sauce is so hot and spicy it may have an aphrodisiac effect on whoever eats it.

Puttanesca Sauce

¼ cup extra virgin olive oil

4 garlic cloves, minced

2 tablespoons capers, drained

1 tablespoon anchovy paste

1 cup Kalamata olives, pitted and
  coarsely chopped

½ teaspoon dried oregano

1 teaspoon red pepper flakes

1 cup chicken broth

One 35-ounce can peeled tomatoes,
  drained and chopped

2 tablespoons tomato paste

Salt and pepper

Filling

1 cup ricotta

1 cup crumbled feta

1 egg

¼ cup chopped parsley

Noodles

8 no-boil noodles, soaked in hot tap
  water for 10 to 15 minutes and
  drained

PREPARE SAUCE

1. In a medium skillet, heat olive oil over medium-high heat. Add garlic, capers, anchovy paste, olives, oregano, and red pepper flakes. Sauté for 1 minute.

2. Add chicken broth, tomatoes, and tomato paste. Bring to a boil. Reduce heat and simmer, uncovered, for 20 to 25 minutes until thickened.

3. Season with salt and pepper.

PREPARE FILLING

4. In a small bowl, combine ricotta, feta, egg, and parsley. Stir until well blended.

5. Preheat oven to 375°F.

6. Spray an 8 × 8 × 2-inch baking dish with nonstick cooking spray.

LAYER BY LAYER ASSEMBLY

7. Spread a thin layer of sauce on the bottom of the dish. Cover sauce with two noodles, slightly overlapping.

8. Dot top of noodles with one-third of the cheese filling. Spread with a generous layer of sauce.

9. Repeat layers until filling is used up. End with noodles. Top with a generous amount of sauce. *Advance prep completed.* (Can be assembled one day in advance. Cover and refrigerate overnight. Let lasagna come to room temperature before baking.)

BAKING

10. Cover with foil and bake for 40 to 45 minutes. Remove foil and continue to bake for 10 to 15 minutes. Remove from the oven. Let rest 10 to 15 minutes before serving.

SERVES 4 TO 6

Arugula and Prosciutto Lasagna

〜〜〜

One of my favorite pizzas in Italy is made from this combination of fresh arugula and prosciutto. This lasagna spotlights these two flavors nestled between delicate crepes and béchamel.

Sauce
3-cup Béchamel Sauce (page 14)

"Noodles"
12 Crepes (page 10)

Filling
8 ounces fresh mozzarella, sliced
    thin
¼ pound prosciutto, sliced thin
3 cups arugula, a few sprigs reserved
    for top
½ cup grated pecorino Romano, plus
    some for serving

1. Preheat oven to 375°F.
2. Spray an 11×7×1½-inch baking dish with nonstick baking spray.

LAYER BY LAYER ASSEMBLY

3. Spread a layer of sauce on the bottom of the dish. Place three crepes on the bottom of the pan, slightly overlapping.

4. For the filling, place one-third of the mozzarella over the noodles, one-third of the prosciutto over the mozzarella, one-third of the arugula over the prosciutto. Top with ½ cup of the sauce and sprinkle with pecorino.

5. Cover with three more crepes and make another mozzarella/prosciutto/arugula/ sauce/pecorino layer as above.

6. Again, cover with three more crepes and make another mozzarella/prosciutto/ arugula/sauce/pecorino layer. Top with three remaining crepes.

7. Top with remaining sauce and pecorino, and reserved arugula for garnish. *Advance prep completed.* (Can be prepared one day in advance. Cover and refrigerate. Let lasagna come to room temperature before baking.)

BAKING

8. Cover with foil and bake for 35 to 40 minutes. Remove foil and continue to bake for 10 to 12 minutes until top is golden brown. Remove from the oven and let cool for 10 to 15 minutes before serving. Serve with additional pecorino.

SERVES 4

Lasagne Quattro Stagione

~~~

Celebrate each of the four seasons with this one lasagna. Each quarter spotlights seasonal ingredients to give this lasagna a striking presentation.

Sauces
Quick Tomato Sauce (page 16)
3-cup Béchamel Sauce (page 14)

Filling
6 ounces sliced portobella
    mushrooms, cleaned and sliced and
    sautéed in 2 tablespoons olive oil
One 14-ounce can artichoke hearts,
    drained and diced
1 large zucchini, sliced into rounds
    and sautéed in ¼ cup olive oil
½ pound sweet Italian sausage,
    casings removed, sautéed until
    brown and drained of grease
1 cup grated pecorino Romano
8 ounces fresh mozzarella, cut into
    small pieces

Noodles
16 no-boil noodles, soaked in hot tap
    water for 10 to 15 minutes, and
    drained

1. Preheat oven to 375°F.
2. Spray a 13 × 9 × 3-inch baking dish with nonstick cooking spray.

LAYER BY LAYER ASSEMBLY
3. Spread a layer of tomato sauce on the bottom of the dish. Top with four noodles, slightly overlapping. Top with a generous layer of Béchamel Sauce.

4. On top of the béchamel, you are going to create four individual sections of the first four fillings. Think of them as four individual rectangles, each containing a different "seasonal" ingredient. On the upper right-hand corner, arrange one-third of the mushrooms in the first rectangle. Working clockwise, arrange one-third of the artichokes on half of the two noodles just below them to create the second rectangle. To the left of the artichoke segment, arrange one-third of the zucchini to create the third rectangle, and above that create the final rectangle by covering it with one-third of the sausage. Sprinkle with one-third of the pecorino and mozzarella.

5. Make two more layers as specified in step 4, but reserve a few slices of each ingredient for the top last layer.

6. Top with remaining four noodles and tomato sauce, placing one or two pieces of mushroom, artichoke, zucchini, and sausage on top of the appropriate area. *Advance prep completed.* (Can be assembled one day in advance. Cover and refrigerate overnight. Let lasagna come to room temperature before baking.)

BAKING

7. Cover with foil and bake for 40 to 45 minutes. Remove foil and continue to bake for an additional 10 to 15 minutes. Remove from the oven. Let rest 10 to 15 minutes before serving.

SERVES 6 TO 8

Sausage Mushroom Lasagna
with Pink Sauce

~~~~~~

This main-dish lasagna is a full-bodied combination of sausage, mushrooms, and cheese with a creamy pink tomato sauce. If you'd like a little spice, you can substitute hot sausage instead of sweet sausage.

Sauce

2 pounds sweet Italian sausage,
    casings removed

1 pound mushrooms, sliced

Salt and pepper

¼ cup finely diced onion

¼ cup dry white wine

Two 35-ounce cans plum tomatoes,
    crushed by hand

2 tablespoons tomato paste

¼ cup heavy cream

Filling

1 egg

1 pound ricotta

½ cup grated pecorino Romano

2 cups shredded mozzarella

Noodles

16 no-boil noodles, soaked in hot tap
    water for 10 to 15 minutes and
    drained

PREPARE SAUCE

1. Heat a large skillet over medium-high heat. Add sausage and cook for about 5 minutes. Use a wooden spoon to break the sausage into small pieces as it cooks. Cook until done. Remove sausage with a slotted spoon and set aside.

2. Add mushrooms to pan. Season with salt and pepper. Cook, stirring occasionally, until well browned. Remove mushrooms with slotted spoon and set aside.

3. Add onion to pan and stir for 2 minutes.

4. Add wine. Using a wooden spoon, scrape up browned bits on bottom of pan. Cook 2 to 3 minutes.

5. Add tomatoes and tomato paste. Return sausage and mushrooms to the pan.

Bring to a boil. Reduce heat and simmer, uncovered, stirring occasionally, for 20 to 25 minutes until reduced.

6. Stir in cream.

PREPARE FILLING

7. In a medium bowl, combine all filling ingredients. Mix until blended.

8. Preheat oven to 375°F.

9. Spray a 13×9×3-inch baking dish with nonstick cooking spray.

LAYER BY LAYER ASSEMBLY

10. Spread a layer of sauce on the bottom of the dish. Top with four noodles, slightly overlapping.

11. Dot with one-third of the cheese filling. Spread with another layer of sauce.

12. Repeat layers until all noodles and filling are used up.

13. Cover the top layer of noodles with a generous amount of sauce. *Advanced prep completed.* (Can be assembled one day in advance. Cover and refrigerate overnight. Let lasagna come to room temperature before baking.)

BAKING

14. Cover with foil and bake for 40 to 45 minutes. Remove foil and continue to bake for an additional 10 to 15 minutes. Remove from the oven. Let rest 10 to 15 minutes before serving.

SERVES 6 TO 8

Sausage and Broccoli Rabe Lasagna with Spicy Tomato Sauce

～～～

Using no-boil noodles makes this satisfying and hearty weekday supper a snap to prepare. Broccoli rabe is a bitter green, here perfectly paired with sausage and a spicy red pepper–laced tomato sauce.

Sauce

1 pound hot Italian sausage, casings removed

1 bunch broccoli rabe, rinsed and coarsely chopped

Salt and pepper

1 tablespoon red pepper flakes

2 cups chicken broth

6 ounces tomato paste

½ cup grated pecorino Romano

Noodles

12 no-boil noodles, soaked in hot tap water for 10 to 15 minutes and drained

PREPARE SAUCE

1. Heat a large skillet over medium heat. Add sausage to skillet. Using a wooden spoon, break up pieces of sausage. Cook sausage until cooked through.

2. Add broccoli rabe, salt, pepper, red pepper flakes, and ½ cup of chicken broth. Cover and cook until broccoli rabe is tender, about 3 minutes.

3. Add remaining broth and tomato paste. Bring to a boil. Reduce heat and cook for 5 to 10 minutes.

4. Preheat oven to 375°F.

5. Spray an 8 × 8 × 2-inch baking dish with nonstick baking spray.

LAYER BY LAYER ASSEMBLY

6. Spread a thin layer of sauce on the bottom of the dish. Cover with three noodles, slightly overlapping.

7. Top with a layer of sauce and a sprinkle of pecorino.

8. Repeat layers until all noodles and sauce are used up.

9. Cover top noodles with a generous amount of sauce. Top with pecorino. *Advance prep completed*. (Can be assembled one day in advance. Cover and refrigerate. Bring to room temperature before baking.)

BAKING

10. Cover with foil and bake for 45 to 50 minutes. Remove foil and bake for 10 to 15 minutes. Remove from the oven. Let rest 10 to 15 minutes before serving.

SERVES 4

Lazy Carbonara Penne for a Crowd

~~~

This rich "lazy" lasagna is the perfect comfort food. It makes a great make-ahead dish, perfect for a large holiday gathering. It's become a New Year's Day tradition at our house, served with roast pork tenderloin.

Undercook the penne, as it will continue to cook while baking.

Sauce
10-Cup Béchamel Sauce (page 14)

"Noodles"
4 pounds penne, slightly
    undercooked and drained

Filling
2 pounds pancetta, diced
6 garlic cloves, minced
1 cup white wine
1 cup chopped parsley
1½ cups grated Parmesan
1 cup grated pecorino Romano
Salt and pepper

PREPARE FILLING
1. In a medium skillet, cook the pancetta.
2. Add garlic. Add wine and cook for an additional 2 minutes. Stir in parsley and salt and pepper.
3. Preheat oven to 375°F.
4. Butter an 18 × 13½ × 3-inch baking dish.

LAYER BY LAYER ASSEMBLY
5. Spread a layer of Béchamel Sauce on the bottom of the dish. Add half the pasta to the pan.
6. Top with half the remaining sauce and half the pancetta mixture.

7. Sprinkle with half of the Parmesan and pecorino. Top with remaining pasta.

8. Top with remaining pancetta mixture, sauce, and cheeses. *Advance prep completed.* (Can be prepared one day in advance. Cover and refrigerate overnight. Let lasagna come to room temperature before baking.)

BAKING

9. Cover with foil and bake for 50 to 60 minutes. Remove foil and bake for 10 to 15 minutes. Remove from the oven. Let rest 10 to 15 minutes before serving.

SERVES 20 TO 25

Smaller Version

Sauce
4-Cup Béchamel Sauce (page 14)

"Noodles"
1 pound penne, slightly undercooked
     and drained

Filling
½ pound pancetta, diced
2 garlic cloves, minced
½ cup white wine
¼ cup chopped parsley
½ cup grated Parmesan
½ cup grated pecorino Romano
Salt and pepper

Follow same directions as for larger version.

Spray a 13×9×3-inch baking dish with nonstick cooking spray. Decrease baking time to 20 to 30 minutes, covered with foil, and an additional 10 to 15 minutes uncovered. Let rest 10 to 15 minutes before serving.

SERVES 6 TO 8

"Lazy Lasagna" with Vodka Sauce

Growing up, we always called this dish of baked macaroni "lazy lasagna." I'm not sure what is lazy about this, because you still have to make sauce and filling, boil pasta, and bake! Rigatoni has always been a favorite pasta, but you can use another such as penne, small shells, or ziti if you prefer. Slightly undercook the pasta, as it will continue to cook while baking.

Vodka Sauce
¼ cup extra virgin
   olive oil
4 garlic cloves, smashed
¼ cup chopped parsley
½ cup vodka
One 35-ounce can peeled tomatoes,
   crushed by hand
Salt and pepper
½ cup heavy cream

Filling
2 cups ricotta
2 eggs
½ cup grated pecorino Romano, plus
   extra for serving
2 cups shredded mozzarella
2 tablespoons chopped parsley
Salt and pepper

"Noodles"
1 pound rigatoni, slightly
   undercooked and drained

PREPARE SAUCE

1. In a large skillet over medium-high heat, heat olive oil. Add garlic and cook for 1 minute.

2. Add parsley and vodka. Cook for 1 minute.

3. Add tomatoes. Season with salt and pepper. Bring to a boil. Reduce heat and simmer, uncovered, for 15 to 20 minutes until thickened.

4. Stir in cream. Remove from heat. Set aside. (Sauce can be made in advance. Refrigerate or freeze without adding the cream. When reheating, add the cream.)

PREPARE FILLING

5. In a mixing bowl, combine ricotta, eggs, pecorino, mozzarella, parsley, and salt and pepper. Stir until blended.

6. Preheat oven to 375°F.

7. Spray a 13 × 9 × 3-inch baking dish with nonstick cooking spray.

LAYER BY LAYER ASSEMBLY

8. Spread a layer of sauce on the bottom of the dish. Top with one-third of the pasta. Top with half the filling.

9. Spread with another layer of sauce.

10. Repeat layering with pasta, filling, sauce, and pasta. Cover top pasta with a generous amount of sauce. *Advance prep completed.* (Can be prepared one day in advance. Cover and refrigerate overnight. Let lasagna come to room temperature before baking.)

BAKING

11. Cover with foil and bake for 35 to 40 minutes. Remove foil and bake for another 10 to 15 minutes. Remove from the oven. Let rest 10 to 15 minutes before serving. Serve with additional pecorino.

SERVES 6 TO 8

Paglia e Fieno
(Straw and Hay) Lasagna

~~~

This is another favorite pasta dish translated to a unique lasagna. The name "straw and hay" refers to the mixture of regular noodles and spinach noodles. This lasagna is not only tasty, but makes a striking presentation topped with a layer of green and white noodles.

Sauce

4-Cup Béchamel Sauce (page 14)

Filling

15 slices prosciutto, thinly sliced

1½ cups frozen peas

1 cup grated Parmesan

Noodles

6 to 8 pieces of Fresh Egg Pasta (page 4), cooked according to directions on page 6

6 to 8 pieces of Spinach Pasta, made with 2 eggs (page 14)

1. Preheat oven to 375°F.
2. Spray a 10×6×3-inch baking dish with nonstick cooking spray.

LAYER BY LAYER ASSEMBLY

3. Spread a layer of sauce on the bottom of the dish. Place two spinach noodles on the bottom of the dish, slightly overlapping.

4. Top with a piece of prosciutto, sprinkle with peas, then Parmesan.

5. Spread a layer of sauce. Top with a layer of egg noodles, slightly overlapping.

6. Repeat layers until noodles and filling are used up, about six layers of noodles and five layers of filling. Be sure to save one noodle of each, the egg and the spinach, for the top. Cover top noodles with a generous amount of sauce. Sprinkle with Parmesan. *Advance prep completed.* (Can be prepared one day in advance. Cover and refrigerate overnight. Let lasagna come to room temperature before baking.)

BAKING

7. Cover with foil and bake for 35 to 40 minutes. Remove foil and continue to bake for an additional 10 to 15 minutes. Remove from the oven. Let rest 10 to 15 minutes until serving.

SERVES 6 TO 8

Lasagna Quattro Formaggi

This lasagna of "four cheeses" is the ultimate Italian mac and cheese. It's the perfect flavorful prima piatti for just about any meal. Prima piatti translates to "first plate," meaning it's a good first-course pasta followed by some type of grilled meat and vegetable. One of the best things about Italian dining is lingering between courses. It is equally tasty with no-boil noodles or home-made noodles.

Sauce

1 cup crumbled Gorgonzola

1 cup grated pecorino Romano, plus
   ¼ cup additional pecorino for
   the top

3-Cup Béchamel Sauce (page 14)

Filling

16 ounces mozzarella, sliced

1 cup shredded Asiago

2 tablespoons chopped basil

Noodles

14 no-boil noodles, soaked in hot tap
   water for 10 to 15 minutes and
   drained

or

Fresh Egg Pasta (page 4), cooked
   according to directions on page 6

PREPARE SAUCE

1. Stir Gorgonzola and pecorino into hot béchamel. Over low heat, stir until cheese is melted. Set aside.

2. Preheat oven to 375°F.

3. Spray an 8×8×2-inch baking dish with nonstick cooking spray.

LAYER BY LAYER ASSEMBLY

4. Spread a thin layer of sauce on the bottom of the dish. Top with two noodles, slightly overlapping. Sprinkle with mozzarella and Asiago.

5. Spread another layer of sauce. Place two noodles on top, slightly overlapping.

6. Repeat layers until all noodles and sauce are used up, ending with noodles.

7. Cover top noodles with a generous amount of sauce.

8. Top with pecorino and chopped basil. *Advance prep completed.* (Can be prepared a day in advance. Cover and refrigerate overnight. Bring to room temperature before baking.)

BAKING

9. Cover with foil and bake for 40 to 45 minutes. Remove foil and continue to bake for an additional 10 to 15 minutes. Remove from the oven. Let rest 10 to 15 minutes before serving.

SERVES 4 TO 6

Carnevale Lasagna

~~~

This loaded lasagna is made to celebrate Mardi Gras, or Fat Tuesday. It is filled with mini meatballs, hard-boiled eggs, béchamel, and rich tomato sauce. It's meant to be the last big splurge before the fasting and sacrifice of Lent. It features two sauces, one with tomato and meatballs, and another béchamel. These sauces, as well as the filling of hard-boiled eggs, can be made one day in advance, then assembled.

Meatballs
1 pound ground beef
1 cup fresh bread crumbs
1 egg
2 tablespoons chopped parsley
¼ cup grated pecorino Romano
Salt and pepper
¼ cup olive oil

Sauce
½ cup chopped onion
2 garlic cloves, minced
½ cup dry red wine
One 28-ounce can peeled tomatoes,
    crushed by hand
2-Cup Béchamel Sauce (page 14)

Filling
6 hard-boiled eggs, sliced crosswise
1 cup grated pecorino Romano

Noodles
16 no-boil noodles, soaked in hot tap
    water for 10 to 15 minutes and
    drained
or
Fresh Egg Pasta (page 4), cooked
    according to directions on page 6

PREPARE MEATBALLS AND SAUCE

1. In a medium mixing bowl, combine ground beef, bread crumbs, egg, parsley, pecorino, and salt and pepper. Mix until blended.

2. Roll into ½-inch balls.

3. In a large skillet, heat ¼ cup olive oil. Working in batches, add the meatballs and cook until done, 5 to 10 minutes. Using a slotted spoon, remove meatballs from the pan.

4. Add onion and garlic to the pan and cook until onion is tender, 3 to 5 minutes.

5. Add wine. Use a wooden spoon to scrape up all the browned bits from the bottom of the pan.

6. Add tomatoes and bring to a boil. Reduce heat and simmer until thickened, 10 to 15 minutes.

7. Preheat oven to 375°F.

8. Spray a 13 × 9 × 3-inch baking dish with nonstick cooking spray.

LAYER BY LAYER ASSEMBLY

9. Spread a layer of tomato sauce on the bottom of the dish. Top with four noodles, slightly overlapping.

10. Place one-third of the meatballs and the two sliced eggs on top of noodles.

11. Top with béchamel, tomato sauce, and pecorino. Top with four noodles, slightly overlapping.

12. Repeat layers until all meatballs, egg slices, and pecorino are used up.

13. Cover top noodles with a generous helping of sauce. *Advance prep completed.* (Can be prepared one day in advance. Cover and refrigerate overnight. Bring lasagna to room temperature before baking.)

BAKING

14. Cover with foil and bake for 45 to 50 minutes. Remove foil and continue to bake for an additional 10 to 15 minutes. Remove from the oven. Let rest 10 to 15 minutes before serving.

SERVES 6 TO 8

Lasagna alla Norma

Alla Norma *is a popular flavor in Sicily and refers to anything with eggplant. Broiling the slices of eggplant before assembling the lasagna gives them a nice roasted flavor and makes the baking time for the lasagna a bit less. Be sure to salt the eggplant to get rid of any bitterness.*

Filling
2 small eggplants, peeled, sliced thin, salted, and drained (see Note)
½ cup grated pecorino Romano
2 cups shredded mozzarella

Noodles
12 no-boil noodles, soaked in hot tap water for 10 to 15 minutes and drained

Sauce
Quick Tomato Sauce (page 16)

PREPARE FILLING
1. Preheat broiler.
2. Place eggplant slices in a single layer on a cookie sheet.
3. Broil 3 to 4 minutes just until tender. Let cool.
4. Reduce the oven heat to 375°F.
5. Spray an 8 × 8 × 2-inch baking dish with nonstick cooking spray.

LAYER BY LAYER ASSEMBLY
6. Spread a layer of sauce on the bottom of the dish. Top with two noodles, slightly overlapping.
7. Top with slices of eggplant. Sprinkle one-quarter of pecorino and of mozzarella.
8. Spread with a layer of sauce.
9. Repeat layers until noodles, eggplant, and cheese are used up, about four layers, three noodles each layer.

Lasagna Bolognese, page 46

Lasagna Caprese, page 90

Chicken Pesto Lasagna, page 128

Beet Lasagna with Creamy Gorgonzola Sauce, page 108

Lazy Carbonara Penne for a Crowd,
page 66

Quick Black Bean Tortilla Lasagna, page 106

Lasagna Primavera
(bottom), page 80; Arugula
and Prosciutto Lasagna
(top), page 58

10. Cover top noodles with a generous amount of sauce and mozzarella. *Advance prep completed.* (Can be prepared one day in advance. Cover and refrigerate overnight. Let lasagna come to room temperature before baking.)

BAKING

11. Cover with foil and bake for 40 to 50 minutes. Remove foil and continue to bake for an additional 10 to 15 minutes. Remove from the oven. Let rest 10 to 15 minutes before serving.

SERVES 4

How to Get Rid of Bitterness in Eggplant

Cut eggplant into slices (peeled or unpeeled, as desired). Sprinkle slices with a generous amount of salt. Place in a colander. Let rest for 30 minutes. Pat eggplant dry before proceeding with recipe.

Winter Lasagna

~~~

My good friend Tom Butcher's flavorful braised lamb shanks become the filling of this satisfying free-form lasagna. Pair with a hearty red wine, crusty bread, and green salad for a comforting winter meal. This lasagna is versatile and delicious made with wonton wrappers, fresh pasta, or layers of polenta. It actually tastes better the day after it is made. After shredding the lamb, cool meat and sauce to room temperature. Refrigerate overnight in an airtight container and simply reheat the following evening.

Sauce and Filling

¼ cup extra virgin olive oil

Salt and pepper

2 large lamb shanks (about
  1½ pounds each)

1 medium onion, cut into
  ¼-inch pieces

1 large carrot, diced into ¼-inch pieces

2 celery stalks, cut into ¼-inch
  pieces

2 garlic cloves, minced

1 bay leaf

2 thyme sprigs

1 rosemary sprig

½ cup dry vermouth

One 28-ounce can peeled tomatoes,
  crushed by hand, with juice

Noodles

8 no-boil noodles, soaked in hot tap
  water for 10 to 15 minutes,
  drained, and each cut in half

Shaved Parmigiano-Reggiano

PREPARE SAUCE AND FILLING

1. Preheat oven to 350°F.
2. In a large Dutch oven, heat olive oil over high heat.

3. Salt and pepper the lamb shanks generously. Sear the shanks on each side until well browned. Remove shanks from the pot.

4. Add onions to pot and cook for 1 to 2 minutes. Add carrots, celery, and garlic. Cook for 1 to 2 minutes.

5. Add the bay leaf, thyme, and rosemary and cook for 1 minute. Add vermouth. Use a wooden spoon to scrape any browned bits from the bottom of the pot.

6. Add tomatoes. Return shanks to pan. Bring to a boil. Cover pot with foil, then place lid on top of foil.

7. Bake for 3 hours.

8. Remove lamb shanks from the sauce. With a fork, shred the meat and discard the bones. Return the shredded meat to the sauce. Remove and discard bay leaf and rosemary and thyme sprigs. (Sauce can be prepared one to two days in advance. Cool, cover, and refrigerate.)

9. Preheat oven to 200°F.

10. Place ovenproof plates in oven until ready to assembly lasagnas, for 10 to 15 minutes. Carefully remove when ready to assemble.

11. Be sure that sauce and filling are hot. This will help to cook the pasta and make it tender.

LAYER BY LAYER ASSEMBLY

12. Spoon sauce on plate. Top with a piece of pasta. Spoon sauce over pasta. Top with another layer of pasta. Continue to layer sauce, pasta, sauce, and pasta. Top with more sauce and shaved Parmesan.

17. Place assembled lasagnas in oven until serving, about 5 minutes.

SERVES 4

Lasagna Primavera

This lasagna is quite labor-intensive, but well worth the effort. It has two delicious fillings, one with a combination of three cheeses and another with flavorful seasonal vegetables. The fresh flavor of dill added to the cheese filling makes this dish an ideal one for Easter or any spring celebrations.

Sauce

4-Cup Béchamel Sauce (page 14)

Cheese Filling

2 cups ricotta

1 egg

2 tablespoons chopped dill, plus
  some for garnish

¼ cup grated pecorino Romano, plus
  some for serving

½ cup cubed fontina

Salt and pepper

Vegetable Filling

2 tablespoons butter

¼ cup chopped shallots

2 cups finely chopped carrots

1 bunch asparagus, cut into ½-inch
  pieces

One 14-ounce can artichoke hearts,
  drained and chopped

Salt and pepper

1 cup vegetable broth

Noodles

12 pieces Fresh Egg Pasta (page 4),
  cooked according to directions on
  page 6

PREPARE CHEESE FILLING

1. In a medium mixing bowl, combine ricotta, egg, dill, ¼ cup pecorino, and fontina. Mix until well blended. Season with salt and pepper. Set aside.

PREPARE VEGETABLE FILLING

2. In a large skillet, over medium heat, melt butter. When foam subsides, add shallots. Cook for 2 to 3 minutes, being careful not to brown them.

3. Add carrots, asparagus, and artichoke hearts. Season with salt and pepper.

4. Add vegetable broth. Bring to a boil. Cover, reduce heat, and simmer for 10 to 12 minutes.

5. Preheat oven to 375°F.

6. Spray a 13×9×3-inch baking dish with nonstick cooking spray.

LAYER BY LAYER ASSEMBLY

7. Spread a layer of sauce on the bottom of the dish. Line the bottom of the dish with three noodles, slightly overlapping.

8. Top with one-third of the cheese filling and one-third of the vegetable filling. Spread a layer of sauce completely over the vegetable and cheese fillings.

9. Top with noodles, slightly overlapping. Top with another third of the cheese filling and another third of vegetable filling. Once again, spread a layer of sauce over all the fillings.

10. Top with noodles. Spread remaining third of the cheese and vegetable fillings evenly over the top. Spread a layer of sauce over the filling.

11. Top with noodles, slightly overlapping. Top with the remaining sauce. Sprinkle with additional pecorino. *Advance prep completed.* (Can be prepared one day in advance. Cover and refrigerate overnight. Bring to room temperature before baking.)

BAKING

12. Cover with foil and bake for 45 to 50 minutes. Remove foil and continue to bake for an additional 10 to 15 minutes. Remove from the oven. Let rest 10 to 15 minutes before serving. Garnish with chopped dill and serve with pecorino.

SERVES 6 TO 8

Late Summer Lasagna

This dish utilizes the late summer abundance of farm-fresh zucchini, basil, and tomatoes. It is a perfect side dish paired with grilled meats or sausages. If you're really short on time, pick up a jar of pesto from your local gourmet store.

Sauce
Pesto Sauce (page 17)

Filling
1 medium zucchini, sliced thin
2 ripe tomatoes, sliced thin
8 ounces fresh mozzarella, sliced thin

Noodles
6 no-boil noodles, soaked for 10 to 15 minutes in hot tap water and drained
¼ cup grated pecorino Romano

1. Preheat oven to 375°F.
2. Spray an 8 × 8 × 2-inch baking dish with nonstick cooking spray.

LAYER BY LAYER ASSEMBLY

3. Spread a thin layer of pesto on the bottom of the dish. Place 2 noodles, slightly overlapping, over pesto.
4. Top with zucchini, tomato, and mozzarella slices.
5. Top with pesto and noodles.
6. Repeat layers until all noodles and filling are used up, about three layers of two noodles each layer.
7. Cover top noodles with a layer of pesto and sprinkle with the pecorino.

BAKING

8. Cover with foil and bake for 25 minutes. Remove foil and continue to bake for another 15 minutes. Remove from oven. Let lasagna rest 10 to 15 minutes before serving.

SERVES 4

Autumn Pancetta and Porcini Lasagna

~~~~

This untraditional lasagna uses whole wheat crepes simply folded over, stacked, and filled with this rich autumn mushroom sauce. Plate them individually for an impressive presentation.

Sauce

¼ pound pancetta, cut into
    small pieces
6 ounces baby bella or button
    mushrooms, sliced
Salt and pepper
¼ cup dry vermouth
1½ cups light cream

Filling

1 ounce dried porcini mushrooms,
    soaked for 10 to 15 minutes in
    1 cup very hot water, drained,
    and chopped

"Noodles"

8 whole wheat crepes (page 12)
¼ cup grated Parmesan

PREPARE SAUCE

1. In a medium skillet, cook pancetta over medium heat until cooked through, 4 to 5 minutes.

2. Add the baby bella or button mushrooms. Season with salt and pepper. Cook for 5 to 8 minutes.

3. Add vermouth. Cook for 1 minute.

4. Add cream. Bring to a boil. Lower heat and simmer for 5 minutes.

PUTTING IT ALL TOGETHER

5. On four warmed plates, spread a small amount of sauce.

6. Top with one crepe. Fill half of crepe with sauce and filling. Fold over crepe. Spoon sauce and filling over this, and repeat with another crepe. Sprinkle with Parmesan. Serve immediately.

SERVES 4

Double Pesto Lasagna

This summer lasagna uses two great pestos, the classic with basil, and a sun-dried tomato and black olive pesto that I fell in love with in Napa, California. Four separate individual lasagnas are baked in the same dish. Use a spatula to remove pieces from the baking dish and serve on individual plates.

Sun-Dried Tomato Pesto
1 jar julienned sun-dried tomatoes
    with olive oil and herbs
½ cup pitted cured black olives
¼ cup torn basil leaves
1 garlic clove

Sauces
Half a recipe Pesto Sauce (page 17)

Filling
8 ounces fresh mozzarella, sliced
    into 12 pieces
½ cup grated pecorino Romano

Noodles
8 no-boil noodles, soaked in hot tap
    water for 10 to 15 minutes and
    drained

PREPARE SAUCE
1. Puree the tomato pesto ingredients in a food processor.
2. Preheat oven to 375°F.
3. Spray a 13×9×3-inch baking dish with nonstick cooking spray.

LAYER BY LAYER ASSEMBLY
4. Cut each noodle in half horizontally. Place four pieces of noodles in bottom of dish, not overlapping or touching.
5. Top each noodle with a tablespoon of sun-dried tomato pesto and a slice of mozzarella.
6. Top each noodle with another piece. Spread a tablespoon of pesto sauce on top.
7. Top with mozzarella.
8. Repeat a layer of noodle, sun-dried tomato pesto, and mozzarella. Top with remaining noodles and pesto sauce.

BAKING

9. Bake, uncovered, for 15 to 20 minutes.

10. Remove lasagnas from baking dish and place on individual warmed plates. Serve immediately.

SERVES 4

Classic Vegetarian Lasagna

This classic lasagna of broccoli, carrots, and onions seemed to be a staple of brunches in the '70s and '80s. It's still a family favorite in our house, even for nonvegetarians.

Sauce
3 tablespoons butter
1 medium onion, chopped
3 carrots, chopped
2 tablespoons flour
2 cups milk
10 ounces frozen chopped broccoli,
    thawed and drained
Salt and pepper

Filling
2 cups ricotta
1 egg
1 cup shredded mozzarella
½ cup grated pecorino Romano
2 tablespoons chopped basil
2 tablespoons chopped parsley
Salt and pepper

Noodles
12 no-boil noodles, soaked in hot tap
    water for 10 to 15 minutes and
    drained

PREPARE SAUCE
1. In a large skillet, melt butter. Add onion and carrots and cook until tender, 3 to 5 minutes.
2. Add flour and stir to coat.
3. Add milk and stir. Bring to a boil.

4. Add broccoli and stir until the mixture is thickened, 3 to 5 minutes. Season with salt and pepper. Set aside.

PREPARE FILLING

5. In a large bowl combine ricotta, egg, mozzarella, pecorino, basil, and parsley. Stir until well blended. Season with salt and pepper.

6. Preheat oven to 375°F.

7. Spray an 8×8×2-inch baking dish with nonstick cooking spray.

LAYER BY LAYER ASSEMBLY

8. Spread a layer of sauce on the bottom of the dish. Top with three noodles, slightly overlapping.

9. Dot with one-third of the ricotta filling. Spread a layer of sauce on top of the filling and top with three additional noodles.

10. Repeat layers until all noodles and filling are used up—four layers of three noodles each. Cover top noodles with a generous layer of sauce. *Advance prep completed.* (Can be prepared one day in advance. Cover and refrigerate overnight. Bring to room temperature before baking.)

BAKING

11. Cover with foil. Bake for 45 to 50 minutes. Remove foil and cook for an additional 10 to 15 minutes. Remove from the oven. Let rest 10 to 15 minutes before serving.

SERVES 4 TO 6

Tortellini Lasagna

~~~

This strange-sounding lasagna is authentic and straight from Bologna, the birthplace of lasagna. It's an interesting and delicious combination of fine fresh pasta noodles filled with béchamel, tortellini, mortadella, and Parmesan. Mortadella is a type of Italian bologna, found in most Italian delis.

Sauce
4-Cup Béchamel Sauce (page 14)

Filling
12 ounces cheese tortellini, boiled according to manufacturer's directions and drained
¾ pound mortadella, cubed
¾ cup grated Parmesan, plus some for serving, optional

Noodles
9 pieces Fresh Egg Pasta (page 4), cooked according to directions on page 6

1. Preheat oven to 375°F.
2. Spray an 8×8×2-inch baking dish with nonstick cooking spray.

LAYER BY LAYER ASSEMBLY

3. Spread a layer of sauce on the bottom of the dish. Top with three noodles, slightly overlapping. Top with half the tortellini, half the mortadella, and one-third of the Parmesan. Top with a layer of sauce.

4. Top with three noodles, slightly overlapping. Top with remaining tortellini and mortadella and one-third of the Parmesan. Top with sauce.

5. Top with three remaining noodles. Spread remaining sauce evenly over the top. Cover with the remaining Parmesan. *Advance prep completed.* (Can be prepared one day in advance. Cover and refrigerate overnight. Bring lasagna to room temperature before baking.)

BAKING

6. Cover with foil. Bake for 40 to 45 minutes. Remove foil and continue to bake for an additional 10 to 15 minutes. Remove from the oven. Let rest 10 to 15 minutes until serving. Serve with additional Parmesan, if desired.

SERVES 6

You can freeze any extra noodles for future use, or break them up and put them in soup.

Lasagna Caprese

These delicious little lasagna stacks are like a cold pasta salad. Be sure to use a high-quality olive oil for drizzling and the season's ripest tomatoes. "Caprese" is from Capri, the beautiful island off the coast of Naples. It is here that the combination of fresh mozzarella, tomato, and basil originated, and where it is perfected. The ruffle-edged pasta is cooked al dente, or firm "to the tooth."

Sauce and Filling
¼ cup extra virgin olive oil, plus
    some for drizzling
1 ripe tomato large, sliced (8 pieces)
8 ounces fresh mozzarella, sliced
8 whole basil leaves, plus 2 table-
    spoons chopped basil for sprinkling
Sea salt and freshly ground pepper

Noodles
3 ruffle-edged (dried) noodles,
    boiled until al dente and drained

LAYER BY LAYER ASSEMBLY
1. Cut each noodle into four equal pieces.
2. Pour 1 tablespoon of olive oil onto each of four small plates.
3. Place one piece of noodle on top of the olive oil. Top with a slice of tomato.
4. Continue to layer:

> Mozzarella
> Basil leaf
> Noodle
> Tomato
> Mozzarella
> Basil leaf
> Noodle

5. Drizzle with olive oil. Season with salt and pepper. Sprinkle with chopped basil.

SERVES 4

New Flavors

Broccoli Lasagna Roll-Ups ✺

Chicken Marsala Lasagna

Asparagus, Goat Cheese,
and Lemon Lasagna ✺

Mac and Cheese
with Broccoli Lasagna ✺

Mexican Chicken
and Mushroom Lasagna

Butternut Squash Lasagna ✺

Artichoke and Spinach Lasagna ✺

Quick Black Bean Tortilla Lasagna ✺

Beet Lasagna
with Creamy Gorgonzola Sauce ✺

Spicy Turkey Polenta Lasagna

Cajun Turkey Lasagna

Turkey Spinach Roll-Ups

Gorgonzola, Spinach,
and Pine Nut Lasagna ✺

Sun-Dried Tomato
and Portobello Lasagna ✺

Bacon, Egg, and Cheese
Breakfast Lasagna

Chinese Pork and Scallion Lasagna

Mixed Seafood Lasagna

Pulled Pork Barbecue Lasagna

Chicken Pesto Lasagna

Middle Eastern Lasagna

Eggplant, Tomato, and
Black Olive Pesto Lasagna ✺

Lobster Lasagna
with Roasted Red Pepper Sauce

Italian Brunch Lasagna ✺

Individual Creamy Mushroom
Lasagnettes ✺

Lasagna with Short Rib Ragu

Grilled Polenta and Vegetable
Lasagnettes ✺

✺ vegetarian

Broccoli Lasagna Roll-Ups

These ruffle-edged roll-ups are a great side-dish lasagna. They are easy to prepare and use just a bit of heavy cream as a sauce. My husband, Edgar, loves them paired with roasted chicken or strip steak.

Sauce
½ cup heavy cream

Noodles
6 ruffle-edged (dried) noodles,
    boiled until al dente and drained

Filling
2 tablespoons butter, plus some for
    topping
½ cup chopped shallots
2 cups chopped broccoli, finely
    chopped
1 cup ricotta
¼ cup grated pecorino Romano
1 egg
Salt and pepper

PREPARE FILLING

1. In a medium skillet, over medium heat, melt the 2 tablespoons butter. Add shallots and broccoli. Cook until tender, about 8 minutes. Let cool.

2. In a small bowl, combine ricotta, pecorino, egg, and salt and pepper. Add cooled broccoli mixture to the cheese mixture.

3. Preheat oven to 375°F.

4. Butter a 9-inch pie dish.

5. Spread about 2 tablespoons of filling at the end of each noodle. Roll noodle and place in the baking dish, seam side down. Top each noodle with a pat of butter and pour cream over the tops. Cover with foil and bake for 20 to 25 minutes.

SERVES 4 TO 6

Chicken Marsala Lasagna

~~~

Everyone's favorite chicken dish becomes this delicious creamy lasagna. Be sure to use a genuine Marsala wine, not a "Marsala-flavored" cooking wine. Real Marsala is the famous Sicilian fortified wine.

Sauce
¼ cup extra virgin olive oil
Two 8-ounce boneless, skinless chicken breasts, cut into small pieces
10 ounces baby bella or button mushrooms, sliced
3 tablespoons butter
3 tablespoons flour
1½ cups Marsala
2 cups heavy cream
Salt and pepper

Filling
¾ cup grated pecorino Romano
1 cup cubed mozzarella

Noodles
12 no-boil noodles, soaked in hot tap water for 10 to 15 minutes and drained

PREPARE SAUCE
1. In a large skillet, heat olive oil over medium-high heat.
2. Add chicken and cook until cooked through.
3. Remove from the pan. Add mushrooms and cook until golden. Remove from the pan.
4. Add butter to pan. When foam subsides, add flour. Stir with a whisk until light brown.
5. Add Marsala. Let cook for 1 minute.
6. Add cream. Bring to a boil. Stir just until thickened. Return chicken and mushrooms to sauce. Season with salt and pepper.

7. Preheat oven to 375°F.

8. Spray an 8×8×2-inch baking dish with nonstick cooking spray.

LAYER BY LAYER ASSEMBLY

9. Spread a layer of sauce on the bottom of the dish. Top with three noodles, slightly overlapping.

10. Top with a layer of sauce. Sprinkle with one-third of the pecorino and mozzarella.

11. Repeat layers until all noodles, cheese, and sauce is used up—about four layers. Cover top noodles with a generous amount of sauce. *Advance prep completed.* (Can be made one day in advance. Cover and refrigerate overnight. Bring to room temperature before baking.)

BAKING

12. Cover with foil and bake for 35 to 40 minutes. Remove foil and continue to bake for an additional 10 to 15 minutes. Remove from the oven. Let rest 10 to 15 minutes before serving.

SERVES 4 TO 6

Asparagus, Goat Cheese,
and Lemon Lasagna

Tangy goat cheese and roasted asparagus combine with zesty lemon in this refreshing lasagna. Try it as part of an Easter buffet. It is delicious using either noodles or crepes. While grating lemon zest, be sure to avoid the white pith of the lemon, which adds bitterness.

1 bunch asparagus
2 tablespoons extra virgin olive oil
Salt and pepper

Sauce
3 tablespoons butter
1½ cups heavy cream
Salt and pepper
Zest of 1 lemon, grated

Filling
1 egg
1½ cups ricotta
4 ounces goat cheese, crumbled
2 tablespoons chopped parsley
Zest of 1 lemon, grated
Salt and pepper

Noodles
8 no-boil noodles, soaked in hot tap
    water for 10 to 15 minutes and
    drained
or
8 to 10 crepes (page 10)

PREPARE ASPARAGUS
1. Preheat oven to 400°F.
2. Spread asparagus on a cookie sheet. Drizzle with the extra virgin olive oil and sprinkle with salt and pepper.

3. Roast at 400°F for 10 to 12 minutes.

4. Cut into 1-inch pieces. Set aside.

PREPARE SAUCE

5. In a medium saucepan, over medium heat, melt butter.

6. Add cream and salt and pepper. Bring to a boil, stirring constantly until thickened.

7. Remove from the heat. Stir in lemon zest. Set aside.

PREPARE FILLING

8. In a medium bowl, combine egg, ricotta, goat cheese, parsley, lemon zest, and salt and pepper. Mix until well blended and smooth.

9. Preheat oven to 375°F.

10. Spray an 8×8×2-inch baking dish with nonstick cooking spray.

LAYER BY LAYER ASSEMBLY

11. Spread a thin layer of sauce on the bottom of the prepared dish. Top with two noodles, slightly overlapping.

12. Dot one-third of the filling on top of the noodles.

13. Spread one-third of the asparagus on top of the filling. Spread a layer of sauce over the asparagus.

14. Repeat layers until all noodles, filling, and asparagus are used up—four layers, two noodles each.

15. Cover top noodles with a generous amount of sauce. *Advance prep completed.* (Can be prepared one day in advance. Cover and refrigerate overnight. Let come to room temperature before baking.)

BAKING

16. Cover with foil. Bake for 25 to 30 minutes. Remove foil and continue to bake for another 5 to 10 minutes. Remove from the oven. Let rest 10 to 15 minutes before serving.

SERVES 4 TO 6

Mac and Cheese with Broccoli Lasagna

All-American mac and cheese stars with broccoli in this lasagna. A creamy Cheddar sauce blankets the noodles and hides the broccoli nestled between. A pinch or two of cayenne pepper spices up this classic. It's a perfect side-dish lasagna paired with grilled pork chops or a home-style meatloaf.

4 cups broccoli, cut into large pieces

Sauce
2 tablespoons flour
1 teaspoon salt
1 teaspoon dry mustard
⅛ teaspoon black pepper
¼ teaspoon cayenne pepper
⅛ teaspoon nutmeg
2 cups heavy cream
1 egg
½ cup sour cream

Filling
1¼ cups cubed sharp Cheddar
1 cup shredded sharp Cheddar

Noodles
12 no-boil noodles, soaked in hot tap
    water for 10 to 15 minutes and
    drained

PREPARE BROCCOLI
1. Bring a medium pan filled with water to a boil. Add broccoli. Cook for 5 minutes. Drain.

PREPARE SAUCE
2. In a medium saucepan, combine flour, salt, mustard, black pepper, cayenne, and nutmeg. Whisk in heavy cream, egg, and sour cream. Bring to a boil over medium heat. Stir until thickened. Set aside.

3. Preheat oven to 375°F.

4. Butter an 8 × 8 × 2-inch baking dish.

LAYER BY LAYER ASSEMBLY

5. Spread a thin layer of sauce on the bottom of the dish. Top with three noodles, slightly overlapping.

6. For the filling, top with one-third of the cubed cheese and broccoli. Spread a layer of sauce on top of the cheese and broccoli.

7. Top with three noodles, slightly overlapping.

8. Repeat layers until noodles, cheese, and broccoli are used up—four layers of three noodles each. Cover top noodles with a generous amount of sauce. Sprinkle top with shredded cheddar. *Advance prep completed.* (Can be prepared one day in advance. Cover and refrigerate overnight. Let lasagna come to room temperature before baking.)

BAKING

9. Cover with foil and bake 30 to 40 minutes. Remove foil and continue to bake for an additional 10 to 15 minutes. Let rest 10 to 15 minutes before serving.

SERVES 4

Mexican Chicken and Mushroom Lasagna

~~~~~~

Fresh cilantro, chili powder, and oregano give this lasagna its south-of-the-border flavor. Corn tortillas are the perfect "noodles" for this flavorful twist to traditional lasagna. Serve with a dollop of pico de gallo, sour cream, or guacamole.

Sauce

4 tablespoons (½ stick) butter

2 tablespoons olive oil

½ cup finely chopped onions

2 teaspoons chili powder

2 garlic cloves, minced

1 teaspoon dried oregano

8 ounces baby bella or button
    mushrooms, sliced

2 teaspoons flour

2 cups milk

⅔ cup chopped cilantro

Salt and pepper

Filling

2 cups cubed cooked chicken

2 cups shredded Monterey jack

"Noodles"

Twelve 7-inch corn tortillas

PREPARE SAUCE

1. In a large skillet, heat butter and olive oil over medium-high heat until melted. Sauté onion for a few minutes until softened, and add chili powder, garlic, and oregano. Sauté for about 1 minute.

2. Add mushrooms and cook until tender, about 10 minutes. With a slotted spoon, remove mushrooms and set aside.

3. Add flour to skillet and cook until light brown. Add milk. Stir with a wooden spoon until sauce begins to thicken. Stir in cilantro and salt and pepper. Set aside.

4. Preheat oven to 375°F.

5. Spray an 8×8×2-inch baking dish with nonstick cooking spray.

LAYER BY LAYER ASSEMBLY

6. Spread a thin layer of sauce on the bottom of the dish. Line the dish with three tortillas, slightly overlapping.

7. Spread a layer of sauce on top of the tortillas. Spread chicken, mushrooms, and cheese on top of sauce.

8. Top with tortillas, slightly overlapping.

9. Repeat layers until all chicken, mushrooms, cheese, and tortillas are used up—four layers of three tortillas each.

10. Cover top tortilla with a generous amount of sauce. *Advance prep completed.* (Can be prepared one day in advance. Cover and refrigerate. Let lasagna come to room temperature before baking.)

BAKING

11. Cover with foil. Bake for 30 to 40 minutes. Remove foil and bake for an additional 5 to 10 minutes. Remove from the oven. Let rest 5 minutes before serving.

SERVES 4

Butternut Squash Lasagna

Roasted butternut squash with sage and onions gives this autumn lasagna an amazing flavor. It's a perfect first course for a Thanksgiving feast.

Sauce
4-Cup Béchamel Sauce (page 14)

Filling
4 cups peeled cubed butternut
    squash
8 sage leaves
1 small onion, sliced
Salt and pepper
¼ cup extra virgin olive oil
1 cup ricotta
1 egg
¼ cup grated Parmesan

Noodles
8 to 10 pieces of Fresh Egg Pasta
    (page 4)
¼ cup grated Parmesan

PREPARE FILLING

1. Preheat oven to 375°F.

2. Place squash, sage, and onion in a baking dish. Season with salt and pepper. Drizzle with olive oil. Roast for 25 to 30 minutes until squash is tender. Remove from oven and cool. Turn off the oven.

3. Place cooled squash mixture in a food processor and puree until smooth. (Can be made two to three days in advance. Cover and refrigerate until using.)

4. Add ricotta, egg, and Parmesan to the squash mixture. Mix until well blended.

5. Preheat oven to 375°F.

6. Spray a 10×10×2-inch baking dish with nonstick cooking spray.

LAYER BY LAYER ASSEMBLY

7. Spread a thin layer of sauce on the bottom of the dish. Top with two noodles, slightly overlapping.

8. Spread one-third of filling over noodles. Spread a thin layer of sauce over filling.

9. Repeat layers until all filling and noodles are used up—about four layers.

10. Cover top noodles with a generous helping of sauce. Sprinkle top with Parmesan. *Advance prep completed.* (Can be assembled one day in advance. Cover and refrigerate. Let lasagna come to room temperature before baking.)

BAKING

11. Cover with foil and bake for 45 to 50 minutes. Remove foil and bake for an additional 10 minutes. Remove from the oven. Let it rest 10 to 15 minutes before serving.

SERVES 6 AS A MAIN DISH OR 8 TO 10 AS AN APPETIZER

Artichoke and Spinach Lasagna

Another great prima piatti *or "first-course" lasagna, this combination of artichoke, spinach, and garlic is a popular one. Making the filling is as easy as tossing a salad. Just be sure to gently press down onto layers of noodles as you assemble this lasagna. The filling will reduce and cook down during baking.*

Sauce
3-Cup Béchamel Sauce (page 14)

Filling
6 ounces fresh spinach, coarsely
    chopped
One 14-ounce can artichoke hearts,
    drained and coarsely chopped
2 garlic cloves, minced
Salt and pepper
1 cup grated pecorino Romano

Noodles
12 no-boil noodles, soaked in hot tap
    water for 10 to 15 minutes and
    drained

PREPARE FILLING

1. In a large bowl, combine spinach, artichokes, garlic, and salt and pepper. Toss to mix.
2. Preheat oven to 375°F.
3. Spray an 11 × 7 × 1½-inch baking dish with nonstick cooking spray.

LAYER BY LAYER ASSEMBLY

4. Spread a thin layer of sauce on the bottom of the dish. Top with three noodles, slightly overlapping.
5. Place one-third of the spinach mixture on top of the noodles. Spread a layer of sauce on top of the filling. Sprinkle with ¼ cup of pecorino.

6. Top with three noodles, slightly overlapping.

7. Repeat layers until noodles, filling, and most of the pecorino are used up—four layers. Cover top noodles with a generous layer of sauce. Sprinkle with remaining pecorino.

BAKING

8. Cover with foil and bake for 25 to 30 minutes. Remove foil and bake for another 10 to 15 minutes until top is browned. Remove from the oven. Let rest 10 to 15 minutes before serving.

SERVES 4

Quick Black Bean
Tortilla Lasagna

This lasagna is a quick way to satisfy a craving for Mexican flavors. It's a snap to prepare using store-bought salsa and black beans. It's a perfectly easy summer lunch served al fresco.

Sauce
2 cups tomato salsa

"Noodles"
Four 7-inch flour tortillas

Filling
One 15-ounce can black beans,
   rinsed and drained
1 cup shredded Cheddar

Topping
2 tablespoons chopped cilantro
Salsa, sour cream, and guacamole
   for serving

1. Preheat oven to 375°F.
2. Spray a 9-inch baking dish with nonstick cooking spray.

LAYER BY LAYER ASSEMBLY

3. Spread a thin layer of salsa on bottom of dish. Place one tortilla over salsa.
4. Top with one-third of the salsa, and a little less than one-third of the black beans and Cheddar.
5. Top with one tortilla.
6. Continue to layer with remaining beans, salsa, and Cheddar, using about 2 heaping tablespoons of each for each layer of filling. Repeat layers until all filling and tortillas are used up—four layers.
7. Cover top tortilla with a generous layer of salsa and Cheddar.

BAKING

8. Bake, uncovered, for 45 to 50 minutes. Remove from the oven.

9. Using a large spatula, remove lasagna from the baking dish and place on a serving dish, if desired. Sprinkle with chopped cilantro.

10. Serve with additional salsa, sour cream, and guacamole.

SERVES 2 AS A MAIN DISH OR 4 AS AN APPETIZER

Beet Lasagna with Creamy Gorgonzola Sauce

The colorful beet pasta of this lasagna pairs well with a simple rich Gorgonzola sauce. Topped with walnuts that roast while baking, this lasagna is sure to satisfy.

Sauce

2 tablespoons butter

2 tablespoons extra virgin olive oil

3 garlic cloves, minced

8 ounces Gorgonzola, broken into
small pieces (3 or 4 small pieces
reserved for topping)

2 cups heavy cream

2 tablespoons chopped basil

Noodles

8 to 10 pieces Beet Pasta (page 9)

½ cup medium-size pieces walnuts

PREPARE SAUCE

1. In a large skillet, heat butter and olive oil over medium heat. Add garlic. Cook for about 30 seconds or until just beginning to brown.

2. Add Gorgonzola and cream. Stir until cheese is melted and sauce is thickened. Remove from the heat and stir in basil.

3. Preheat oven to 375°F.

4. Spray an 11 × 7 × 1½-inch baking dish with nonstick cooking spray.

LAYER BY LAYER ASSEMBLY

5. Spread a layer of sauce on the bottom of the dish. Top with two noodles, slightly overlapping.

6. Repeat layers until all noodles and sauce are used up. Cover top noodles with a generous helping of sauce.

7. Sprinkle the top with walnuts. *Advance prep completed.* (Can be prepared one day in advance. Cover and refrigerate overnight. Bring to room temperature before baking.)

BAKING

8. Cover with foil and bake for 25 to 30 minutes. Remove foil and bake for an additional 5 to 10 minutes. Remove from the oven. Sprinkle with reserved Gorgonzola pieces. Let rest 10 to 15 minutes before serving.

SERVES 6

Spicy Turkey Polenta Lasagna

~~~

Instant polenta, made from coarse cornmeal, and an easy spicy meat sauce make this lasagna a snap to prepare. The polenta is cut into squares that act as the noodles. Try our Thanksgiving turkey leftover variation. It's a tasty way to use up all that turkey.

Sauce
2 tablespoons extra virgin olive oil
1 garlic clove, minced
1 teaspoon red pepper flakes
½ pound ground turkey
Salt and pepper
One 28-ounce can diced tomatoes, drained
2 ounces tomato paste

Filling
1½ cups shredded mozzarella
½ cup grated pecorino Romano

"Noodles"
4 cups salted water
1 cup instant polenta
2 tablespoons grated pecorino Romano

PREPARE POLENTA

1. Bring salted water to a boil.
2. Gradually whisk in polenta and continue to whisk until thick, about 2 minutes.
3. Whisk in pecorino.
4. Pour into greased 13×9×3-inch pan. Let cool. Cover with plastic wrap and refrigerate for 1 to 2 hours or overnight. The polenta cannot be cut until it has thoroughly cooled and set. (Can be made two days ahead.)
5. Cut into eight equal pieces, each about four inches square.

PREPARE SAUCE

6. In a large skillet over medium-high heat, heat olive oil. Add garlic and red pepper flakes. Sauté for 1 minute.
7. Add turkey and season with salt and pepper. Stir occasionally until turkey is cooked through.

8. Add tomatoes and tomato paste. Bring to a boil. Reduce heat and simmer, uncovered, until thick, 15 to 20 minutes.

9. Preheat oven to 375°F.

10. Spray an 8×8×2-inch baking dish with nonstick cooking spray.

LAYER BY LAYER ASSEMBLY

11. Spread a layer of sauce on the bottom of the baking dish. Lay half the polenta squares over sauce, slightly overlapping.

12. Top with a layer of sauce, half of the mozzarella, and half of the pecorino.

13. Top with another layer of polenta, slightly overlapping.

14. Cover top with a generous amount of sauce and remaining cheeses. *Advance prep completed.* (Can be prepared one day in advance. Cover and refrigerate. Let lasagna come to room temperature before baking.)

BAKING

15. Bake for 30 to 40 minutes until bubbly. Remove from the oven. Let rest 10 to 15 minutes before serving.

SERVES 4 TO 6

Thanksgiving Turkey Leftover

Prepare sauce as directed above without ground turkey. When sauce is done, stir in 3 cups cubed cooked turkey.

Cajun Turkey Lasagna

~~~

This spicy lasagna is perfect for big appetites and a Super Bowl buffet. It's loaded with andouille sausage, Cajun spices, turkey, and Cheddar. Try it for tailgating!

Sauce

1 pound turkey cutlets, cut into
   ½-inch pieces

3 teaspoons Cajun Dry Rub (recipe
   follows)

2 tablespoons extra virgin olive oil

1 pound andouille sausage, thinly
   sliced

1 small onion, chopped

2 garlic cloves, minced

1 small green cubanelle pepper,
   chopped

2 celery stalks, chopped

3 cups half-and-half

6 ounces tomato paste

2 cups shredded Cheddar cheese

"Noodles"

Eight 9-inch flour tortillas

PREPARE SAUCE

1. In a small mixing bowl, toss turkey pieces with dry rub to coat.

2. In a large skillet, heat olive oil over medium-high heat. Cook sausage and turkey until cooked through, 5 to 6 minutes. Using a slotted spoon, remove meat from the skillet. Set aside.

3. In the same skillet, sauté onion, garlic, cubanelle pepper, and celery until tender.

4. Return sausage and turkey to the pan.

5. Add half-and-half and tomato paste. Stir until thickened.

6. Preheat oven to 375°F.

7. Spray an 11 × 7 × 1½-inch baking dish with nonstick cooking spray.

LAYER BY LAYER ASSEMBLY

8. Spread a layer of sauce on the bottom of the pan. Top with two tortillas, slightly overlapping.

9. Top tortillas with a layer of sauce and one-third of the Cheddar.

10. Top with two tortillas, slightly overlapping.

11. Repeat layers until the tortillas and cheese are used up, making four layers in all.

12. Cover top tortillas with a generous amount of sauce. *Advance prep completed.* (Can be prepared one day in advance. Cover and refrigerate overnight. Bring lasagna to room temperature before baking.)

BAKING

13. Cover with foil and bake for 40 to 45 minutes. Remove foil and bake for an additional 10 to 15 minutes. Remove from the oven. Let rest 10 to 15 minutes before serving.

SERVES 6

Cajun Dry Rub

There are many great dry rubs readily available in most supermarkets, but here's a recipe for a favorite homemade rub. You can use it to season the pork in the Pulled Pork Barbecue Lasagna (page 126), too.

1 teaspoon white pepper

1 teaspoon onion powder

½ teaspoon garlic powder

1 teaspoon dried thyme

1 teaspoon celery seed

½ teaspoon cayenne pepper

¼ teaspoon salt

In a small bowl, combine all ingredients. Stir to mix in spices. Use immediately or store in an airtight container at room temperature.

Turkey Spinach Roll-Ups

~~~~~

The filling and sauce for these lasagna roll-ups can be made in advance, then assembled for impressive individual lasagnas.

Sauce
¼ cup extra virgin olive oil
1 onion, diced
2 garlic cloves, minced
1 pound ground turkey
One 28-ounce can peeled tomatoes,
   crushed by hand
Salt and pepper

Noodles
12 ruffle-edged (dried) noodles,
   boiled until al dente and drained

Filling
1½ cups ricotta
¼ cup grated pecorino Romano, plus
   2 tablespoons
1 egg
½ cup shredded mozzarella
One 10-ounce package frozen
   spinach, thawed, chopped, and
   drained

PREPARE SAUCE
1. In a large skillet, over medium-high heat, heat olive oil. Add onion and cook until tender, about 5 minutes.

2. Add garlic. Cook for another minute.

3. Add turkey and cook, stirring until meat is cooked through.

4. Add tomatoes. Bring to a boil. Season with salt and pepper. Boil, uncovered, until sauce is thickened, 10 to 15 minutes.

5. In a medium bowl, combine ricotta, pecorino, egg, mozzarella, and spinach. Mix until blended.

6. Preheat oven to 375°F.

7. Spray a 13×9×3-inch baking dish with nonstick cooking spray.

8. Place 2 tablespoons of filling in each noodle. Roll up.

9. Place lasagnas seam side down in baking dish.

10. Top with sauce and an additional 2 tablespoons of pecorino.

11. Bake, uncovered, for 30 to 35 minutes.

SERVES 6

Thanksgiving Turkey Leftover

Prepare sauce as directed above without ground turkey. When sauce is done, stir in 5 cups of cubed cooked turkey.

Gorgonzola, Spinach, and Pine Nut Lasagna

Gorgonzola delivers full flavor in this vegetarian lasagna. Gorgonzola is a creamy blue-veined Italian cheese. Toasting the pine nuts for this lasagna is easy and brings out the flavor of the nut by releasing the oils. Simply spread pine nuts on a parchment-lined cookie sheet and bake at 400°F for 5 to 8 minutes until lightly browned.

Creamy Gorgonzola Sauce (page 108)

Noodles
12 no-boil noodles, soaked in hot tap water for 10 to 15 minutes and drained

Filling
3 tablespoons olive oil
2 garlic cloves, minced
16 ounces fresh spinach
Salt and pepper
½ cup pine nuts, toasted (see headnote), reserve 1 tablespoon for top

PREPARE FILLING

4. Heat olive oil in a large skillet. Add garlic and cook until garlic just begins to brown, 30 to 40 seconds.

5. Add spinach and salt and pepper.

6. Cover pan and wilt spinach, 2 to 3 minutes.

7. Preheat oven to 375°F.

8. Spray an 8 × 8 × 2-inch baking dish with nonstick cooking spray.

9. Spread a thin layer of sauce on the bottom of the dish. Top with three noodles, overlapping.

10. Top with one-third of the spinach and one-quarter of the pine nuts. Spread a layer of sauce over the spinach.

11. Top with noodles.

12. Repeat layers until all noodles and filling are used up, making four layers in all.

13. Cover top noodles with a generous amount of sauce. Top with remaining pine nuts.

BAKING

14. Cover with foil and bake for 30 to 35 minutes. Remove foil and continue to bake for an additional 10 to 15 minutes. Remove from the oven. Let rest 10 to 15 minutes before serving.

SERVES 4

Sun-Dried Tomato and Portobello Lasagna

For this easy robust lasagna look for julienned sun-dried tomatoes packed in oil with herbs. Cut into small squares, this can be an appetizer lasagna.

Sauce

¼ cup olive oil

10 ounces baby bella mushrooms, sliced

One 8.5-ounce jar julienned sun-dried tomatoes packed in oil with herbs, drained

2 tablespoons tomato paste

2 cups light cream

½ cup grated pecorino Romano

Noodles

12 no-boil noodles, soaked in hot tap water for 10 to 15 minutes, and drained

PREPARE SAUCE

1. In a large skillet, heat olive oil over medium heat. Sauté mushrooms until tender, 8 to 10 minutes.

2. Add sun-dried tomatoes. Stir in tomato paste and cream. Bring to a boil. Reduce heat and simmer for 5 minutes or until the sauce is thickened. Remove from heat.

3. Preheat oven to 375°F.

4. Spray an 8×8×2-inch baking dish with nonstick cooking spray.

LAYER BY LAYER ASSEMBLY

5. Spread a layer of sauce on the bottom of the dish. Top with two noodles, slightly overlapping. Top with a layer of sauce. Sprinkle with pecorino.

6. Repeat layers until all noodles, sauce, and pecorino are used up, making six layers.

Cover top noodles with a generous amount of sauce. *Advance prep completed.* (Can be prepared one day in advance. Cover and refrigerate overnight. Let lasagna come to room temperature before baking.)

BAKING

7. Cover with foil and bake for 40 to 45 minutes. Remove foil and continue to bake for an additional 10 to 15 minutes. Remove from the oven. Let rest 10 to 15 minutes before serving.

SERVES 4 AS A MAIN DISH OR 8 AS AN APPETIZER

Bacon, Egg, and Cheese
Breakfast Lasagna

~~~

Classic American breakfast fare turns into a yummy breakfast lasagna. The preparation is definitely more like a strata. Cheddar and bacon are layered with white bread, eggs, and milk to create a silky sauce. Assemble this strata in the evening and enjoy a tasty breakfast or brunch in the morning.

Sauce
6 eggs
2 cups milk
1 teaspoon salt
1 teaspoon pepper

"Noodles"
6 slices white bread

Filling
2 cups shredded Cheddar cheese
½ pound bacon, cooked and broken
    into small pieces

PREPARE SAUCE

1. In a medium bowl, combine eggs, milk, and salt and pepper. Whisk until well blended. Set aside.

2. Spray an 11×7×1½-inch baking dish with nonstick cooking spray.

LAYER BY LAYER ASSEMBLY

3. Layer three bread slices, slightly overlapping, into bottom of the dish. Sprinkle with half the cheese and all of the bacon. Place three remaining bread slices on top. Sprinkle with cheese.

4. Pour sauce over the top of the lasagna. Cover with plastic wrap and refrigerate overnight. Remove from the refrigerator 30 minutes before baking.

BAKING

5. Preheat oven to 375°F. Remove plastic wrap, cover with foil, and bake 40 to 45 minutes. Remove foil and bake for an additional 10 minutes or until a tester inserted into the center comes out clean. Remove from the oven. Let rest 5 to 10 minutes before serving.

SERVES 6

Chinese Pork and Scallion Lasagna

~~~

Lasagna goes Asian with this flavorful dish created with the help of my friend Richard Lee. We've taken his classic Chinese secret sauce and layered it with tender egg roll wrappers and a flavorful pork and scallion filling. Most of these ingredients are available in large supermarkets or Asian markets.

Even if the egg roll wrappers stick together after boiling, you can still piece them together to layer like noodles. Use fresh ginger for the fullest flavor.

Sauce
½ cup soy sauce
1 tablespoon sesame oil
1½ teaspoons Asian barbecue paste
2 teaspoons chili paste

"Noodles"
15 egg roll wrappers, blanched and
    drained

Filling
1 pound ground pork
½ cup chopped scallions, plus some
    for garnish
1 cup chopped Napa cabbage
1 egg
2 tablespoons soy sauce
½ teaspoon grated fresh ginger
1 tablespoon tapioca

PREPARE SAUCE

1. In a small bowl, whisk all sauce ingredients until blended.

PREPARE FILLING

2. In a medium bowl, combine all filling ingredients. Mix until thoroughly blended.

3. Preheat oven to 375°F.

4. Spray an 8 × 8 × 2-inch baking dish with nonstick cooking spray.

LAYER BY LAYER ASSEMBLY

5. Spread a thin layer of sauce on the bottom of the dish. Top with a layer of three egg roll wrappers, slightly overlapping.

6. Top with one-quarter of the pork filling. Spread a layer of sauce on top of the filling.

7. Repeat layers until all egg roll wrappers and filling are used up, about five layers. Cover the top wrappers with sauce. *Advance prep completed.* (Can be assembled one day in advance. Cover and refrigerate overnight. Let lasagna come to room temperature before baking.)

BAKING

8. Cover with foil and bake for 50 to 55 minutes. Remove foil and continue to bake for an additional 5 to 10 minutes. Be sure that pork is cooked through. Remove from the oven. Let lasagna rest 10 to 15 minutes before serving.

9. Serve sprinkled with additional scallions.

SERVES 4 TO 6 AS A MAIN DISH OR 8 TO 10 AS AN APPETIZER

Mixed Seafood Lasagna

~~~~~~

Shrimp, scallops, and crabmeat star in this delicately flavored seafood lasagna. Seafood is a tricky thing to add to lasagna. While making the filling be sure not to overcook it, as it will cook again in the noodles.

Sauce
3-Cup Béchamel Sauce (page 14)

Filling
1 tablespoon olive oil
2 tablespoons butter
2 tablespoons chopped shallots
1 teaspoon thyme
2 tablespoons chopped parsley, plus
    additional for topping
¾ pound small shrimp, tails
    removed, peeled, and deveined
¾ pound bay scallops
¾ pound jumbo lump crabmeat
Salt and pepper
¼ cup sherry
½ cup grated Parmesan

Noodles
12 no-boil noodles, soaked in hot tap
    water for 10 to 15 minutes and
    drained

PREPARE FILLING

1. In a large skillet over medium heat, heat olive oil and butter. Add shallots and cook for 1 to 2 minutes, being careful not to brown them. Add thyme and parsley.

2. Add seafood and cook, stirring occasionally, until almost cooked through. Season with salt and pepper.

3. Add sherry. Cook for 1 minute.

4. Preheat oven to 375°F.

5. Butter an 8×8×2-inch baking dish.

LAYER BY LAYER ASSEMBLY

6. Spread a layer of sauce on the bottom of the dish. Top with three noodles, overlapping.

7. Spread one-third of the filling, then a layer of sauce, on top of the noodles. Top with another layer of noodles.

8. Repeat layers until all noodles and filling are used up, making four layers. Cover top noodles with a generous amount of sauce. Top with Parmesan and parsley.

BAKING

9. Cover with foil and bake for 20 to 25 minutes. Remove foil and bake for an additional 10 minutes. Remove from the oven. Let rest 10 to 15 minutes before serving.

SERVES 4

Pulled Pork Barbecue Lasagna

~~~~~

One of my favorite food groups, Southern barbecue, is featured in this lasagna. Serve with slaw, the Tennessee way. Although the sauce takes three hours to cook, the rest of the assembly of this lasagna is easy. Make the sauce one day ahead and then just pull it together for a unique week-end supper.

Sauce
2 pounds country-style pork ribs
3 tablespoons Cajun Dry Rub
  (page 112)
Salt and pepper
2 tablespoons olive oil
1 large onion, diced
12 ounces beer
2 cups ketchup
¼ cup cider vinegar
1 tablespoon dry mustard
¼ cup Worcestershire sauce
1 teaspoon salt
1 tablespoon chili powder
2 tablespoons molasses
¼ cup water

Filling
2 cups shredded sharp Cheddar,
  ½ cup reserved for topping

"Noodles"
Eight 7-inch flour tortillas

PREPARE SAUCE
1. Toss ribs with dry rub and salt and pepper.
2. In a Dutch oven, heat olive oil over medium-high heat.
3. Sear ribs on each side. Remove from the pot.
4. Add onion to the pot and cook for 1 to 2 minutes.

5. Add beer and bring to a boil. Using a wooden spoon, scrape up any browned bits on the bottom of the pot.

6. Add ketchup, vinegar, mustard, Worcestershire sauce, salt, chili powder, molasses, and water.

7. Return ribs to the pan. Bring to a boil. Simmer, uncovered, stirring occasionally, for about 3 hours.

8. Remove ribs from the pot. Using two forks, take the meat off the bone.

9. Return shredded meat to the sauce. Discard bones and fat. (Can be prepared one day in advance. Cover and refrigerate.) Before reheating, skim fat off the top and discard.

10. Preheat oven to 375°F.

11. Spray an 11 × 7 × 1½-inch baking dish with nonstick cooking spray.

LAYER BY LAYER ASSEMBLY

12. Spread a thin layer of sauce on the bottom of the dish. Line the dish with two flour tortillas, slightly overlapping.

13. Top with a layer of sauce and one-third of the Cheddar. Top with two flour tortillas.

14. Repeat layers until all tortillas and Cheddar are used up, making four layers.

15. Cover top tortillas with a generous amount of sauce.

16. Top with remaining Cheddar. *Advance prep completed.* (Can be prepared one day in advance. Cover and refrigerate. Bring to room temperature before baking.)

BAKING

17. Cover with foil. Bake for 30 to 35 minutes. Remove foil and continue to bake for an additional 10 to 12 minutes. Remove from the oven. Let rest 10 to 15 minutes before serving.

SERVES 4

Chicken Pesto Lasagna

~~~

Creamy béchamel and flavorful basil pesto combine with chicken and fresh mozzarella in one of my favorite lasagnas. This flavor combination is a definite crowd-pleaser. It's easy to prepare, especially if you start with store-bought pesto and precooked chicken breast.

Sauce
3-cup Béchamel Sauce (page 14)
Pesto Sauce (page 17)

Noodles
16 no-boil noodles, soaked in hot tap
    water for 10 to 15 minutes and
    drained

Filling
4 cups cubed cooked chicken breast
4 or 5 fresh tomatoes, sliced
12 ounces fresh mozzarella, sliced
¼ cup grated pecorino Romano, plus
    some for serving

1. Preheat oven to 375°F.
2. Spray a 13×9×3-inch baking dish with nonstick cooking spray.

LAYER BY LAYER ASSEMBLY

3. Spread a layer of béchamel over the bottom of the dish. Line the pan with four noodles, slightly overlapping. Top with a layer of one-third of the chicken, then tomatoes, mozzarella, pesto, and pecorino.

4. Spread a layer of béchamel over the filling. Top with noodles, slightly overlapping.

5. Repeat layers until all noodles and fillings are used up, making four layers of four noodles each layer. Cover top with a generous layer of béchamel. Sprinkle with pecorino. *Advance prep completed.* (Can be prepared one day in advance. Cover and refrigerate. Bring lasagna to room temperature before baking.)

BAKING

6. Cover with foil. Bake for 35 to 40 minutes. Remove foil and continue to bake for 10 to 15 minutes. Remove from the oven. Let rest 10 to 15 minutes before serving. Serve with additional pecorino.

SERVES 4 TO 6

Middle Eastern Lasagna

~~~

This tasty lasagna has nicely spiced meat and tangy feta cheese filling. The phyllo layers are a crispy surprise. This lasagna is equally good made either with ground sirloin or ground lamb. Cut into small squares, it can be part of a meze, or "small plates" sampling, along with olives, dips, and grilled meats, often served in the Mediterranean.

Sauce
¼ cup extra virgin olive oil
1 large onion, chopped
2 pounds ground sirloin or ground lamb
Salt and pepper
2 teaspoons ground cumin
1 teaspoon ground allspice
6 ounces tomato paste

Filling
8 ounces feta, broken into small
    pieces
3 cups ricotta
2 eggs
¼ cup chopped parsley, plus sprigs
    for topping

"Noodles"
16 sheets phyllo, thawed if frozen
6 tablespoons butter, or more if
    needed, melted and cooled

PREPARE SAUCE

1. In a large skillet, heat olive oil over medium heat. Add onion and sauté for 3 to 4 minutes.

2. Add sirloin, salt and pepper, cumin, and allspice. Cook until meat is done, stirring often.

3. Add tomato paste. Cook until the sauce is thickened, 3 to 5 minutes.

PREPARE FILLING

4. In a bowl, combine the feta, ricotta, eggs, and parsley. Stir until well blended.
5. Preheat oven to 375°F.
6. Coat a 13×9×3-inch baking dish with melted butter.

LAYER BY LAYER ASSEMBLY

7. Line the bottom of the dish with four sheets of phyllo. Be sure to cover remaining sheets of phyllo with a damp kitchen towel until you use them, as they dry out easily.
8. Brush melted butter over phyllo in dish.
9. Dot the top of phyllo with one-third of the filling. Spread a layer of sauce over the filling and top sauce with four sheets of phyllo. Brush with butter.
10. Continue to layer in the following order until you have run out of filling and sauce.

Filling

Sauce

Phyllo

Butter

Filling

Sauce

Phyllo

11. Brush top with butter.
12. Using a sharp knife, score the top sheets of phyllo into squares.
13. Place a small sprig of parsley in the center of each square. *Advance prep completed.* (Can be prepared one day in advance. Cover and refrigerate overnight. Bring to room temperature before baking.)

BAKING

14. Cover with foil and bake for 30 to 40 minutes. Remove foil and continue baking for 10 to 15 minutes until top is golden brown. Remove from the oven. Let rest 5 to 10 minutes before serving.

SERVES 6 TO 8

Eggplant, Tomato, and Black Olive Pesto Lasagna

Using fresh plum tomatoes straight from the garden makes this lasagna taste like summer. If these are not available, you can certainly use canned tomatoes. The pungent black olive pesto layered between these noodles is equally tasty tossed over linguine or chicken.

Sauce
¼ cup extra virgin olive oil
3 cups cubed eggplant (page 76)
2 garlic cloves, minced
2 pounds fresh plum tomatoes,
    blanched, peeled, and chopped
    (see box on page 134)
Salt and pepper

Black Olive Pesto
1 cup pitted cured black olives
1 garlic clove
¼ cup torn basil leaves
2 tablespoons pine nuts
½ cup extra virgin olive oil

8 ounces mozzarella, sliced thin
¼ cup grated ricotta salata, plus
    some for serving

Noodles
8 no-boil noodles, soaked in hot tap
    water for 10 to 15 minutes and
    drained

PREPARE SAUCE

1. In a large skillet, heat extra virgin olive oil over medium heat. Add eggplant and cook, stirring frequently, until tender, about 10 minutes.

2. Add garlic. Add tomatoes. Season with salt and pepper. Bring to a boil and reduce heat. Simmer, uncovered, 10 to 15 minutes. Set aside.

PREPARE PESTO

3. In a food processor, combine olives, garlic, basil, and pine nuts. Pulse until chopped.

4. Add olive oil in a steady stream and mix until blended. (Pesto can be made three to four days in advance. Cover and refrigerate.)

5. Preheat oven to 375°F.

6. Spray an 8 × 8 × 2-inch baking dish with nonstick baking spray.

LAYER BY LAYER ASSEMBLY.

7. Spread a layer of sauce to coat the bottom of the dish. Place two noodles, slightly overlapping, on the bottom of the dish.

8. Place mozzarella slices over noodles and dot with one-third of the black olive pesto.

9. Spread a layer of sauce over filling. Top with two additional noodles.

10. Repeat layers until all noodles and fillings and pesto are used up, about four layers of two noodles each.

11. Top with the sauce, then the ¼ cup ricotta salata. *Advance prep completed.* (Can be prepared one day in advance. Cover and refrigerate overnight. Bring lasagna to room temperature before baking.)

BAKING

12. Cover with foil and bake for 35 to 40 minutes. Remove foil and continue to bake for an additional 10 to 12 minutes. Remove from the oven. Let rest 10 to 15 minutes before serving. Serve with additional grated ricotta salata.

SERVES 4

To Prepare Fresh Plum Tomatoes

Bring a large pot of boiling, salted water to a boil. Drop in 2 pounds of ripe plum tomatoes. Boil for 2 minutes. Remove from water. Cool tomatoes slightly. Peel skin off tomatoes. Slice, chop, or puree.

Lobster Lasagna with Roasted Red Pepper Sauce

~~~~~~

This elegant free-form lasagna for two is a perfect treat for a special celebration. I usually serve it for a low-stress New Year's Eve dinner. After boiling noodles, be sure to save 2 cups of the pasta water to add to the sautéed lobster and red peppers.

Sauce

2 tablespoons butter

2 tablespoons chopped shallots

12 ounces Italian roasted peppers, packed in water, drained, and chopped

6 ounces lobster meat

2 tablespoons chopped parsley

Salt and pepper

Noodles

6 pieces of Fresh Egg pasta (page 4), cooked according to directions on page 6, and cut in half

PREPARE SAUCE

1. In a small skillet, over medium heat, melt butter. When foam subsides, add shallots and cook for 4 to 5 minutes, being careful not to brown them.

2. Add roasted peppers, lobster meat, and parsley.

3. Add salt and pepper. Add pasta water. Lower heat and simmer for 10 to 15 minutes.

4. Spoon sauce onto two heated plates. Top with noodles.

5. Spoon sauce over noodles. Top with noodles, top with sauce, then one more noodle. Serve immediately.

SERVES 2

Italian Brunch Lasagna

Sun-dried tomatoes, spinach, and ricotta fill this lasagna layered with sheets of crispy phyllo. Serve this lasagna for breakfast or brunch, warm or at room temperature.

Filling

One 10-ounce package frozen
    chopped spinach, thawed and
    drained
4 cups ricotta
1 teaspoon chopped parsley
1 teaspoon chopped basil
2 eggs
1 cup grated pecorino Romano, plus
    more for top
½ teaspoon salt
Freshly ground black pepper
1 cup chopped sun-dried tomatoes
8 tablespoons butter (1 stick),
    melted and cooled

"Noodles"

20 sheets phyllo, thawed if frozen

PREPARE FILLING

1. In a mixing bowl, combine spinach, ricotta, parsley, basil, eggs, pecorino, salt, pepper, and sun-dried tomatoes. Mix until blended.
2. Preheat oven to 375°F.
3. Brush a 13×9×3-inch baking dish with melted butter.

LAYER BY LAYER ASSEMBLY

4. Line dish with five layers of phyllo. Cover remaining sheets of phyllo with a damp cloth.
5. Brush phyllo with butter.

6. Spread one-third of the filling over the phyllo.

7. Top with another layer of five sheets of phyllo. Brush with butter.

8. Repeat layers until all filling is used up, making four layers of five sheets each layer.

9. Brush with melted butter and sprinkle with additional pecorino. *Advance prep completed.* (Can be prepared one day ahead. Cover and refrigerate. Bring to room temperature before baking.)

BAKING

10. Cover with foil and bake for 35 to 40 minutes. Remove foil and continue to bake for an additional 10 to 15 minutes until top is golden brown. Remove from the oven. Let rest 10 to 15 minutes before serving.

SERVES 8

Individual Creamy Mushroom Lasagnettes

Simply use soaked no-boil noodles cut in half to make these individual casseroles. The creamy mixed mushroom sauce pairs well with roasted meats as a perfect cold weather meal.

Sauce
2-Cup Béchamel Sauce (page 14)

Filling
2 tablespoons butter

1 medium onion, chopped

10 ounces baby bella mushrooms, coarsely chopped

12 ounces oyster mushrooms, coarsely chopped

¼ cup dry vermouth

Salt and pepper

1 cup shredded mozzarella

½ cup grated pecorino Romano, plus some for serving

Noodles
8 no-boil noodles soaked in hot tap water for 10 to 15 minutes and drained

PREPARE FILLING

1. In a large skillet, over medium heat, melt butter. Add onion and sauté until tender, 3 to 5 minutes.

2. Add baby bella and oyster mushrooms. Cook until tender, about 10 minutes. Add vermouth. Cook for 1 minute. Season with salt and pepper. Set aside.

3. Cut each noodle in half to make a 4-inch square.

4. Preheat oven to 375°F.

5. Spray a 13 × 9 × 3-inch baking dish with nonstick cooking spray.

LAYER BY LAYER ASSEMBLY

6. Spread a small amount of sauce in four areas on the bottom of the dish. Place one pasta square on top of the sauce.

7. Continue to layer mushroom mixture, mozzarella, sauce, and noodles, using four layers of noodles for each individual lasagna.

8. Top with sauce and sprinkle with pecorino Romano. *Advance prep completed.* (Can be prepared one day in advance. Cover and refrigerate overnight. Let come to room temperature before baking.)

BAKING

9. Cover with foil. Bake for 25 to 30 minutes. Remove foil and continue to bake for an additional 5 to 10 minutes. Use a large spatula to transfer lasagnettes to individual plates. Serve with additional pecorino.

SERVES 4

Lasagna with Short Rib Ragu

~~~

This tasty ragu gets its flavor from beef short ribs braised in tomato sauce. A simple layering of the hearty ragu, homestyle noodles, and robust pecorino Romano cheese combine to make this lasagna a satisfying winter supper.

Sauce
Salt and pepper
2 pounds short ribs
¼ cup extra virgin olive oil
½ cup chopped onion
½ cup chopped carrot
½ cup chopped celery
2 garlic cloves, minced
¼ cup red wine
1 cup beef broth
One 35-ounce can peeled tomatoes,
   crushed by hand, with juice

1½ cups grated pecorino Romano,
   plus some for serving

Noodles
10 no-boil noodles, soaked in hot tap
   water for 10 to 15 minutes and
   drained

PREPARE SAUCE
1. Preheat oven to 350°F.

2. Generously salt and pepper the short ribs. In a Dutch oven, heat olive oil over medium-high heat. Sear the ribs on each side. Remove from the pot.

3. Add onions, carrots, celery, and garlic to the pot. Cook for 1 to 2 minutes. Add red wine. Bring to a boil and scrape up any browned bits from the bottom of the pot.

4. Add beef broth and tomatoes. Return short ribs to the pot. Bring to a boil. Cover with foil, then cover with lid. Bake for 2 hours.

5. Remove ribs from the sauce. Using two forks, take the meat off the bone. Return shredded meat to the sauce. Discard bones and fat. (Can be made one day in advance. Refrigerate overnight in an airtight container.)

6. Preheat oven to 375°F.

7. Spray an 8×8×2-inch baking dish with nonstick cooking spray.

LAYER BY LAYER ASSEMBLY

8. Spread a layer of sauce on the bottom of the dish. Top with two noodles, slightly overlapping.

9. Top with a layer of sauce and a generous sprinkle of pecorino.

10. Repeat layers until all noodles and sauce are used up.

11. Cover top noodles with a generous amount of sauce. Sprinkle with pecorino. *Advance prep completed.* (Can be prepared the night before. Cover and refrigerate. Bring to room temperature before baking.)

BAKING

12. Cover with foil and bake for 40 to 45 minutes. Remove foil and continue to bake for an additional 10 to 15 minutes. Remove from the oven. Let rest 10 to 15 minutes before serving. Serve with additional pecorino Romano.

SERVES 4

Grilled Polenta and Vegetable Lasagnettes

Grilled zucchini and fresh mozzarella are the toppings for this open-faced grilled summer lasagna. You can definitely use other summer veggies on the grill such as eggplant, red onion, or tomatoes. The polenta can be made one to two days in advance, or if you're really out of time, use prepared polenta sold in specialty shops. Simply cut polenta into slices about ¼ inch thick.

Filling
1 medium zucchini, sliced thin
   horizontally (12 slices)
1 pound fresh mozzarella,
   sliced thin (12 slices)
Salt and pepper
¼ cup basil leaves, chopped

"Noodles"
2 quarts salted water
2 cups instant polenta
½ cup grated pecorino Romano, plus
   additional for topping
Olive oil for drizzling
Balsamic vinegar

PREPARE POLENTA

1. Bring the water to a boil. Gradually whisk in instant polenta. Whisk 2 to 3 minutes until thickened. Stir in the pecorino.

3. Pour into greased 11×16 cookie sheet. Let cool. Refrigerate overnight. Polenta must be thoroughly cooled and set before it can be cut. Cut into 24 squares.

4. Preheat grill and grill the zucchini slices for 5 minutes on each side.

5. Place polenta squares on grill. Cook until charred on each side, about 5 minutes per side.

6. While polenta is still warm, top with slices of zucchini and mozzarella. Season with salt and pepper.

7. Sprinkle with chopped basil and a drizzle of extra virgin olive oil and balsamic vinegar. Top with another polenta square. Sprinkle with additional pecorino.

8. Serve warm or at room temperature.

SERVES 6 TO 12

Desserts

Orange Ricotta Lasagnettes

Chocolate Tart or Lemon Tart

Frangipane Cake

Date Nut Biscotti

～～～

Generally Italians aren't big dessert eaters. After eating a hearty dinner of lasagna, you may want to serve a simple selection of fruit, biscotti, or sorbet. For something a little more special, try sweet lasagna filled with cream and berries, a delicious chocolate or refreshing lemon tart, or an almond frangipane cake. Pair these desserts with a cup of rich espresso or a light dessert wine.

Orange Ricotta Lasagnettes

~~~~

Ricotta cheese, this time sweetened with sugar and spiked with orange rind and chocolate chips, is the filling for these sweet pastries. You can call them lasagnettes, napoleons, or just delicious! Make an excellent variation using mixed berries.

"Noodles"
1 sheet frozen puff pastry, thawed

Sauce
½ cup chocolate chips, melted

Filling
1 cup ricotta
¾ cup sugar
2 tablespoons minced orange rind

1. Preheat oven to 400°F.

2. Cut pastry into nine 3-inch squares. Place squares on a parchment-lined cookie sheet.

3. Bake until golden brown, 15 to 20 minutes. Remove from the oven. Cool.

4. Combine all filling ingredients in a medium mixing bowl. Stir until well blended.

5. To assemble, split each square in half. Spread a layer of filling on six bottom pieces. Top with another piece of pastry. Spread a layer of filling, and top with another piece of pastry. This will make six three-layer pastries.

6. Drizzle melted chocolate on top of pastries. Refrigerate until serving.

SERVES 6

Mixed Berry Lasagnettes

"Noodles"
1 sheet frozen puff pastry, thawed

Filling
¾ cup heavy cream
3 tablespoons sugar
3 cups mixed berries
Confectioners' sugar

1. Prepare the pastry the same way as you prepared it for the Orange Ricotta Lasagnettes.

2. Whip the heavy cream and sugar together until stiff peaks form. Spread a layer of whipped cream on six bottom pieces of pastry. Top with berries. Top with another piece of pastry. Spread another layer of whipped cream and berries. Top with pastry and dust with confectioners' sugar. Refrigerate until serving.

SERVES 6

Chocolate Tart or Lemon Tart

~~~

These two tarts use the same basic crust. It's a tender crust that you can fill with either a deep rich chocolate ganache, or a light lemon curd. Top each with whipped cream and fresh seasonal fruit such as raspberries or strawberries, and you have the perfect "make-ahead" dessert for any of your lasagna feasts.

Baking the shells ahead of time makes these tarts a snap to prepare. This crust is a favorite of mine because you simply press it into the tart pan. No rolling necessary.

Basic Italian Tart Shell

About 1 cup flour
2 tablespoons confectioners' sugar
Pinch of salt
6 tablespoons unsalted butter, softened
1 egg yolk

Chocolate Ganache Filling

2 cups chocolate chips
1 tablespoon corn syrup
1 tablespoon butter
1 cup heavy cream
1 teaspoon coffee liqueur

Lemon Curd Filling

1 cup sugar
1 tablespoon cornstarch
6 egg yolks
¼ cup lemon juice
1 tablespoon minced lemon rind
¼ pound (1 stick) butter

1. Preheat oven to 375°F.
2. Spray a 9-inch tart pan with removable bottom with nonstick cooking spray.
3. In a food processor combine the flour, sugar, and salt. Add the butter and egg yolk. Pulse until a soft dough forms.
4. Press the dough into the prepared pan.

5. Cover bottom of crust with foil and fill with pie weights or dried beans. Bake for 15 to 20 minutes. Remove foil and weights.

6. Continue to bake for an additional 5 minutes or until lightly browned. Cool before filling.

7. If making the ganache, place chocolate chips, corn syrup, and butter in a small mixing bowl. In a small saucepan over medium heat, heat the cream until boiling. Pour hot cream over chocolate chip mixture. Stir until smooth. Stir in coffee liqueur. Pour into cooled crust. Refrigerate until serving.

FOR LEMON CURD FILLING

7. If making the lemon curd filling, in a small saucepan, combine sugar, cornstarch, egg yolks, lemon juice, and rind.

8. Whisk constantly over medium-high heat until thick. Remove from heat. Add butter. Whisk until butter is melted.

9. Pour into cooled crust. Refrigerate until serving.

Frangipane Cake

~~~~

This dense, moist cake has a light almond taste. It's a classic flavor, accented by any fruit you choose. Top with raspberries, plums, apricots, or slices of pears or apples.

1 pound almond paste, broken into
    small pieces
½ cup sugar
½ cup flour
½ pound (2 sticks) unsalted butter,
    softened

6 eggs
1 cup raspberries or other fruit
    (slices of plum, apricot, pear, or
    apple)
Confectioners' sugar

1. Preheat oven to 350°F. Line a 9-inch cake pan with parchment paper.

2. In an electric mixer, combine the almond paste, sugar, and flour. Mix until blended.

3. Add butter. Mix until smooth.

4. Add eggs, one at a time, beating well after adding each addition.

5. Pour batter into prepared pan. Place raspberries or fruit slices on top.

6. Bake for 45 to 50 minutes until tester comes out of the center with a fine crumb. Cool cake in pan on a wire cooling rack. Remove from pan. Discard parchment. Lightly dust top with confectioners' sugar.

SERVES 8 TO 10

Date Nut Biscotti

Serve these hearty cookies with fresh fruit for a simple Italian dessert. Make a plate that includes biscotti, seasonal fruit, and mellow cheese.

1¼ to 1½ cups flour
1 cup sugar
¼ teaspoon salt
1 teaspoon cinnamon
2 teaspoons baking powder

1 cup chopped dates
1 cup chopped walnuts
3 eggs
3 teaspoons amaretto

1. Preheat oven to 350°F.

2. In a large mixing bowl, combine 1 cup of the flour, the sugar, salt, cinnamon, baking powder, dates, and walnuts.

3. In a separate bowl, whisk the eggs and amaretto with a wire whisk. Pour into the flour mixture. Mix to form a soft dough.

4. Turn the dough out onto a floured surface. Knead in an additional ¼ to ½ cup flour to make a soft but not sticky dough.

5. Divide the dough into three equal pieces. Roll each piece into a loaf about 12 inches long. Place on a parchment-lined cookie sheet, spacing the loaves 4 inches apart. Bake for 20 to 25 minutes until golden brown.

6. While loaves are still slightly warm, slice diagonally into ½-inch cookies. Return cookies to the cookie sheet in a single layer.

Bake for 15 minutes or until toasted. Cool cookies. Store in an airtight container. (Can be frozen up to 1 month in heavy plastic bags.)

MAKES ABOUT 30 BISCOTTI

INDEX